Life Application Bible Studies
HEBREWS

APPLICATION® BIBLE STUDIES

Part 1:
Complete text of Hebrews with study notes and features from the
Life Application Study Bible

Part 2:
Thirteen lessons for individual or group study

Study questions written and edited by

Rev. Neil S. Wilson
Dr. James C. Galvin
Rev. David R. Veerman
Daryl J. Lucas

New Living
Translation

Tyndale House Publishers, Inc.
Carol Stream, Illinois

hebrews

Visit Tyndale's exciting Web site at www.tyndale.com

New Living Translation, NLT, the New Living Translation logo, and *Life Application* are registered trademarks of Tyndale House Publishers, Inc.

Life Application Bible Studies: Hebrews

Copyright © 1999, 2008 by Tyndale House Publishers, Inc., Carol Stream, Illinois 60188. All rights reserved.

Life Application notes and features copyright © 1988, 1989, 1990, 1991, 1993, 1996, 2004 by Tyndale House Publishers, Inc., Carol Stream, Illinois 60188. .

Cover photograph copyright © by iStockphoto. All rights reserved.

The text of Hebrews is from the *Holy Bible,* New Living Translation, copyright © 1996, 2004, 2007 by Tyndale House Foundation. All rights reserved.

ISBN-13: 978-1-4143-2564-4
ISBN-10: 1-4143-2564-9

Printed in the United States of America

14 13 12 11 10 09
7   6   5   4   3   2

CONTENTS

A NOTE TO READERS

The *Holy Bible,* New Living Translation, was first published in 1996. It quickly became one of the most popular Bible translations in the English-speaking world. While the NLT's influence was rapidly growing, the Bible Translation Committee determined that an additional investment in scholarly review and text refinement could make it even better. So shortly after its initial publication, the committee began an eight-year process with the purpose of increasing the level of the NLT's precision without sacrificing its easy-to-understand quality. This second-generation text was completed in 2004 and is reflected in this edition of the New Living Translation. An additional update with minor changes was subsequently introduced in 2007.

The goal of any Bible translation is to convey the meaning and content of the ancient Hebrew, Aramaic, and Greek texts as accurately as possible to contemporary readers. The challenge for our translators was to create a text that would communicate as clearly and powerfully to today's readers as the original texts did to readers and listeners in the ancient biblical world. The resulting translation is easy to read and understand, while also accurately communicating the meaning and content of the original biblical texts. The NLT is a general-purpose text especially good for study, devotional reading, and reading aloud in worship services.

We believe that the New Living Translation—which combines the latest biblical scholarship with a clear, dynamic writing style—will communicate God's word powerfully to all who read it. We publish it with the prayer that God will use it to speak his timeless truth to the church and the world in a fresh, new way.

The Publishers
October 2007

INTRODUCTION TO THE
NEW LIVING TRANSLATION

Translation Philosophy and Methodology

English Bible translations tend to be governed by one of two general translation theories. The first theory has been called "formal-equivalence," "literal," or "word-for-word" translation. According to this theory, the translator attempts to render each word of the original language into English and seeks to preserve the original syntax and sentence structure as much as possible in translation. The second theory has been called "dynamic-equivalence," "functional-equivalence," or "thought-for-thought" translation. The goal of this translation theory is to produce in English the closest natural equivalent of the message expressed by the original-language text, both in meaning and in style.

Both of these translation theories have their strengths. A formal-equivalence translation preserves aspects of the original text—including ancient idioms, term consistency, and original-language syntax—that are valuable for scholars and professional study. It allows a reader to trace formal elements of the original-language text through the English translation. A dynamic-equivalence translation, on the other hand, focuses on translating the message of the original-language text. It ensures that the meaning of the text is readily apparent to the contemporary reader. This allows the message to come through with immediacy, without requiring the reader to struggle with foreign idioms and awkward syntax. It also facilitates serious study of the text's message and clarity in both devotional and public reading.

The pure application of either of these translation philosophies would create translations at opposite ends of the translation spectrum. But in reality, all translations contain a mixture of these two philosophies. A purely formal-equivalence translation would be unintelligible in English, and a purely dynamic-equivalence translation would risk being unfaithful to the original. That is why translations shaped by dynamic-equivalence theory are usually quite literal when the original text is relatively clear, and the translations shaped by formal-equivalence theory are sometimes quite dynamic when the original text is obscure.

The translators of the New Living Translation set out to render the message of the original texts of Scripture into clear, contemporary English. As they did so, they kept the concerns of both formal-equivalence and dynamic-equivalence in mind. On the one hand, they translated as simply and literally as possible when that approach yielded an accurate, clear, and natural English text. Many words and phrases were rendered literally and consistently into English, preserving essential literary and rhetorical devices, ancient metaphors, and word choices that give structure to the text and provide echoes of meaning from one passage to the next.

On the other hand, the translators rendered the message more dynamically when the literal rendering was hard to understand, was misleading, or yielded archaic or foreign wording. They clarified difficult metaphors and terms to aid in the reader's understanding. The translators first struggled with the meaning of the words and phrases in the ancient context; then they rendered the message into clear, natural English. Their goal was to be both faithful to the ancient texts and eminently readable. The result is a translation that is both exegetically accurate and idiomatically powerful.

Translation Process and Team

To produce an accurate translation of the Bible into contemporary English, the translation team needed the skills necessary to enter into the thought patterns of the ancient authors and then to render their ideas, connotations, and effects into clear, contemporary English.

To begin this process, qualified biblical scholars were needed to interpret the meaning of the original text and to check it against our base English translation. In order to guard against personal and theological biases, the scholars needed to represent a diverse group of evangelicals who would employ the best exegetical tools. Then to work alongside the scholars, skilled English stylists were needed to shape the text into clear, contemporary English.

With these concerns in mind, the Bible Translation Committee recruited teams of scholars that represented a broad spectrum of denominations, theological perspectives, and backgrounds within the worldwide evangelical community. Each book of the Bible was assigned to three different scholars with proven expertise in the book or group of books to be reviewed. Each of these scholars made a thorough review of a base translation and submitted suggested revisions to the appropriate Senior Translator. The Senior Translator then reviewed and summarized these suggestions and proposed a first-draft revision of the base text. This draft served as the basis for several additional phases of exegetical and stylistic committee review. Then the Bible Translation Committee jointly reviewed and approved every verse of the final translation.

Throughout the translation and editing process, the Senior Translators and their scholar teams were given a chance to review the editing done by the team of stylists. This ensured that exegetical errors would not be introduced late in the process and that the entire Bible Translation Committee was happy with the final result. By choosing a team of qualified scholars and skilled stylists and by setting up a process that allowed their interaction throughout the process, the New Living Translation has been refined to preserve the essential formal elements of the original biblical texts, while also creating a clear, understandable English text.

The New Living Translation was first published in 1996. Shortly after its initial publication, the Bible Translation Committee began a process of further committee review and translation refinement. The purpose of this continued revision was to increase the level of precision without sacrificing the text's easy-to-understand quality. This second-edition text was completed in 2004, and an additional update with minor changes was subsequently introduced in 2007. This printing of the New Living Translation reflects the updated 2007 text.

Written to Be Read Aloud

It is evident in Scripture that the biblical documents were written to be read aloud, often in public worship (see Nehemiah 8; Luke 4:16-20; 1 Timothy 4:13; Revelation 1:3). It is still the case today that more people will hear the Bible read aloud in church than are likely to read it for themselves. Therefore, a new translation must communicate with clarity and power when it is read publicly. Clarity was a primary goal for the NLT translators, not only to facilitate private reading and understanding, but also to ensure that it would be excellent for public reading and make an immediate and powerful impact on any listener.

The Texts behind the New Living Translation

The Old Testament translators used the Masoretic Text of the Hebrew Bible as represented in *Biblia Hebraica Stuttgartensia* (1977), with its extensive system of textual notes; this is an update of Rudolf Kittel's *Biblia Hebraica* (Stuttgart, 1937). The translators also further compared the Dead Sea Scrolls, the Septuagint and other Greek manuscripts, the Samaritan Pentateuch, the Syriac Peshitta, the Latin Vulgate, and any other versions or manuscripts that shed light on the meaning of difficult passages.

The New Testament translators used the two standard editions of the Greek New Testament: the *Greek New Testament,* published by the United Bible Societies (UBS, fourth revised edition, 1993), and *Novum Testamentum Graece,* edited by Nestle and Aland (NA, twenty-seventh edition, 1993). These two editions, which have the same text but differ in punctuation and textual notes, represent, for the most part, the best in modern textual scholarship. However, in cases where strong textual or other scholarly evidence supported the decision, the translators sometimes chose to differ from the UBS and NA Greek texts and followed variant readings found in other ancient witnesses. Significant textual variants of this sort are always noted in the textual notes of the New Living Translation.

Translation Issues

The translators have made a conscious effort to provide a text that can be easily understood by the typical reader of modern English. To this end, we sought to use only vocabulary and

language structures in common use today. We avoided using language likely to become
quickly dated or that reflects only a narrow subdialect of English, with the goal of making
the New Living Translation as broadly useful and timeless as possible.

But our concern for readability goes beyond the concerns of vocabulary and sentence
structure. We are also concerned about historical and cultural barriers to understanding the
Bible, and we have sought to translate terms shrouded in history and culture in ways that can
be immediately understood. To this end:

- We have converted ancient weights and measures (for example, "ephah" [a unit of
  dry volume] or "cubit" [a unit of length]) to modern English (American) equivalents,
  since the ancient measures are not generally meaningful to today's readers. Then in
  the textual footnotes we offer the literal Hebrew, Aramaic, or Greek measures, along
  with modern metric equivalents.
- Instead of translating ancient currency values literally, we have expressed them in
  common terms that communicate the message. For example, in the Old Testament,
  "ten shekels of silver" becomes "ten pieces of silver" to convey the intended
  message. In the New Testament, we have often translated the "denarius" as "the
  normal daily wage" to facilitate understanding. Then a footnote offers: "Greek *a
  denarius*, the payment for a full day's wage." In general, we give a clear English
  rendering and then state the literal Hebrew, Aramaic, or Greek in a textual footnote.
- Since the names of Hebrew months are unknown to most contemporary readers, and
  since the Hebrew lunar calendar fluctuates from year to year in relation to the solar
  calendar used today, we have looked for clear ways to communicate the time of year
  the Hebrew months (such as Abib) refer to. When an expanded or interpretive
  rendering is given in the text, a textual note gives the literal rendering. Where it is
  possible to define a specific ancient date in terms of our modern calendar, we use
  modern dates in the text. A textual footnote then gives the literal Hebrew date and
  states the rationale for our rendering. For example, Ezra 6:15 pinpoints the date
  when the postexilic Temple was completed in Jerusalem: "the third day of the
  month Adar." This was during the sixth year of King Darius's reign (that is, 515 B.C.).
  We have translated that date as March 12, with a footnote giving the Hebrew and
  identifying the year as 515 B.C.
- Since ancient references to the time of day differ from our modern methods of
  denoting time, we have used renderings that are instantly understandable to the
  modern reader. Accordingly, we have rendered specific times of day by using approx-
  imate equivalents in terms of our common "o'clock" system. On occasion, translations such as "at dawn the next morning" or "as the sun was setting" have been used
  when the biblical reference is more general.
- When the meaning of a proper name (or a wordplay inherent in a proper name) is
  relevant to the message of the text, its meaning is often illuminated with a textual
  footnote. For example, in Exodus 2:10 the text reads: "The princess named him
  Moses, for she explained, 'I lifted him out of the water.' " The accompanying footnote
  reads: "*Moses* sounds like a Hebrew term that means 'to lift out.' "

  Sometimes, when the actual meaning of a name is clear, that meaning is included
  in parentheses within the text itself. For example, the text at Genesis 16:11 reads:
  "You are to name him Ishmael (*which means 'God hears'*), for the LORD has heard
  your cry of distress." Since the original hearers and readers would have instantly
  understood the meaning of the name "Ishmael," we have provided modern readers
  with the same information so they can experience the text in a similar way.
- Many words and phrases carry a great deal of cultural meaning that was obvious
  to the original readers but needs explanation in our own culture. For example, the
  phrase "they beat their breasts" (Luke 23:48) in ancient times meant that people
  were very upset, often in mourning. In our translation we chose to translate this
  phrase dynamically for clarity: "They went home *in deep sorrow.*" Then we included
  a footnote with the literal Greek, which reads: "Greek *went home beating their
  breasts.*" In other similar cases, however, we have sometimes chosen to illuminate
  the existing literal expression to make it immediately understandable. For example,
  here we might have expanded the literal Greek phrase to read: "They went home

beating their breasts *in sorrow."* If we had done this, we would not have included a textual footnote, since the literal Greek clearly appears in translation.

- Metaphorical language is sometimes difficult for contemporary readers to understand, so at times we have chosen to translate or illuminate the meaning of a metaphor. For example, the ancient poet writes, "Your neck is *like* the tower of David" (Song of Songs 4:4). We have rendered it "Your neck is *as beautiful as* the tower of David" to clarify the intended positive meaning of the simile. Another example comes in Ecclesiastes 12:3, which can be literally rendered: "Remember him . . . when the grinding women cease because they are few, and the women who look through the windows see dimly." We have rendered it: "Remember him before your teeth—your few remaining servants—stop grinding; and before your eyes—the women looking through the windows—see dimly." We clarified such metaphors only when we believed a typical reader might be confused by the literal text.

- When the content of the original language text is poetic in character, we have rendered it in English poetic form. We sought to break lines in ways that clarify and highlight the relationships between phrases of the text. Hebrew poetry often uses parallelism, a literary form where a second phrase (or in some instances a third or fourth) echoes the initial phrase in some way. In Hebrew parallelism, the subsequent parallel phrases continue, while also furthering and sharpening, the thought expressed in the initial line or phrase. Whenever possible, we sought to represent these parallel phrases in natural poetic English.

- The Greek term *hoi Ioudaioi* is literally translated "the Jews" in many English translations. In the Gospel of John, however, this term doesn't always refer to the Jewish people generally. In some contexts, it refers more particularly to the Jewish religious leaders. We have attempted to capture the meaning in these different contexts by using terms such as "the people" (with a footnote: Greek *the Jewish people*) or "the religious leaders," where appropriate.

- One challenge we faced was how to translate accurately the ancient biblical text that was originally written in a context where male-oriented terms were used to refer to humanity generally. We needed to respect the nature of the ancient context while also trying to make the translation clear to a modern audience that tends to read male-oriented language as applying only to males. Often the original text, though using masculine nouns and pronouns, clearly intends that the message be applied to both men and women. A typical example is found in the New Testament letters, where the believers are called "brothers" (*adelphoi*). Yet it is clear from the content of these letters that they were addressed to all the believers—male and female. Thus, we have usually translated this Greek word as "brothers and sisters" in order to represent the historical situation more accurately.

  We have also been sensitive to passages where the text applies generally to human beings or to the human condition. In some instances we have used plural pronouns (they, them) in place of the masculine singular (he, him). For example, a traditional rendering of Proverbs 22:6 is: "Train up a child in the way he should go, and when he is old he will not turn from it." We have rendered it: "Direct your children onto the right path, and when they are older, they will not leave it." At times, we have also replaced third person pronouns with the second person to ensure clarity. A traditional rendering of Proverbs 26:27 is: "He who digs a pit will fall into it, and he who rolls a stone, it will come back on him." We have rendered it: "If you set a trap for others, you will get caught in it yourself. If you roll a boulder down on others, it will crush you instead."

  We should emphasize, however, that all masculine nouns and pronouns used to represent God (for example, "Father") have been maintained without exception. All decisions of this kind have been driven by the concern to reflect accurately the intended meaning of the original texts of Scripture.

Lexical Consistency in Terminology

For the sake of clarity, we have translated certain original-language terms consistently, especially within synoptic passages and for commonly repeated rhetorical phrases, and within certain word categories such as divine names and non-theological technical terminology (e.g., liturgical, legal, cultural, zoological, and botanical terms). For theological terms, we have allowed a greater semantic range of acceptable English words or phrases for a single Hebrew or Greek word. We have avoided some theological terms that are not readily understood by many modern readers. For example, we avoided using words such as "justification" and "sanctification," which are carryovers from Latin translations. In place of these words, we have provided renderings such as "made right with God" and "made holy."

The Spelling of Proper Names

Many individuals in the Bible, especially the Old Testament, are known by more than one name (e.g., Uzziah/Azariah). For the sake of clarity, we have tried to use a single spelling for any one individual, footnoting the literal spelling whenever we differ from it. This is especially helpful in delineating the kings of Israel and Judah. King Joash/Jehoash of Israel has been consistently called Jehoash, while King Joash/Jehoash of Judah is called Joash. A similar distinction has been used to distinguish between Joram/Jehoram of Israel and Joram/Jehoram of Judah. All such decisions were made with the goal of clarifying the text for the reader. When the ancient biblical writers clearly had a theological purpose in their choice of a variant name (e.g., Esh-baal/Ishbosheth), the different names have been maintained with an explanatory footnote.

For the names Jacob and Israel, which are used interchangeably for both the individual patriarch and the nation, we generally render it "Israel" when it refers to the nation and "Jacob" when it refers to the individual. When our rendering of the name differs from the underlying Hebrew text, we provide a textual footnote, which includes this explanation: "The names 'Jacob' and 'Israel' are often interchanged throughout the Old Testament, referring sometimes to the individual patriarch and sometimes to the nation."

The Rendering of Divine Names

All appearances of *'el, 'elohim,* or *'eloah* have been translated "God," except where the context demands the translation "god(s)." We have generally rendered the tetragrammaton (*YHWH*) consistently as "the LORD," utilizing a form with small capitals that is common among English translations. This will distinguish it from the name *'adonai,* which we render "Lord." When *'adonai* and *YHWH* appear together, we have rendered it "Sovereign LORD." This also distinguishes *'adonai YHWH* from cases where *YHWH* appears with *'elohim,* which is rendered "LORD God." When *YH* (the short form of *YHWH*) and *YHWH* appear together, we have rendered it "LORD GOD." When *YHWH* appears with the term *tseba'oth,* we have rendered it "LORD of Heaven's Armies" to translate the meaning of the name. In a few cases, we have utilized the transliteration, *Yahweh,* when the personal character of the name is being invoked in contrast to another divine name or the name of some other god (for example, see Exodus 3:15; 6:2-3).

In the New Testament, the Greek word *christos* has been translated as "Messiah" when the context assumes a Jewish audience. When a Gentile audience can be assumed, *christos* has been translated as "Christ." The Greek word *kurios* is consistently translated "Lord," except that it is translated "LORD" wherever the New Testament text explicitly quotes from the Old Testament, and the text there has it in small capitals.

Textual Footnotes

The New Living Translation provides several kinds of textual footnotes, all designated in the text with an asterisk:

- When for the sake of clarity the NLT renders a difficult or potentially confusing phrase dynamically, we generally give the literal rendering in a textual footnote. This allows the reader to see the literal source of our dynamic rendering and how our translation relates to other more literal translations. These notes are prefaced with "Hebrew," "Aramaic," or "Greek," identifying the language of the underlying source text. For example, in Acts 2:42 we translated the literal "breaking of bread" (from the Greek) as "the Lord's Supper" to clarify that this verse refers to the ceremonial practice of the church rather than just an ordinary meal. Then we attached a footnote to "the Lord's Supper," which reads: "Greek *the breaking of bread.*"

- Textual footnotes are also used to show alternative renderings, prefaced with the word "Or." These normally occur for passages where an aspect of the meaning is debated. On occasion, we also provide notes on words or phrases that represent a departure from long-standing tradition. These notes are prefaced with "Tradition-ally rendered." For example, the footnote to the translation "serious skin disease" at Leviticus 13:2 says: "Traditionally rendered *leprosy.* The Hebrew word used throughout this passage is used to describe various skin diseases."

- When our translators follow a textual variant that differs significantly from our stan-dard Hebrew or Greek texts (listed earlier), we document that difference with a foot-note. We also footnote cases when the NLT excludes a passage that is included in the Greek text known as the *Textus Receptus* (and familiar to readers through its transla-tion in the King James Version). In such cases, we offer a translation of the excluded text in a footnote, even though it is generally recognized as a later addition to the Greek text and not part of the original Greek New Testament.

- All Old Testament passages that are quoted in the New Testament are identified by a textual footnote at the New Testament location. When the New Testament clearly quotes from the Greek translation of the Old Testament, and when it differs signifi-cantly in wording from the Hebrew text, we also place a textual footnote at the Old Testament location. This note includes a rendering of the Greek version, along with a cross-reference to the New Testament passage(s) where it is cited (for example, see notes on Proverbs 3:12; Psalms 8:2; 53:3).

- Some textual footnotes provide cultural and historical information on places, things, and people in the Bible that are probably obscure to modern readers. Such notes should aid the reader in understanding the message of the text. For example, in Acts 12:1, "King Herod" is named in this translation as "King Herod Agrippa" and is iden-tified in a footnote as being "the nephew of Herod Antipas and a grandson of Herod the Great."

- When the meaning of a proper name (or a wordplay inherent in a proper name) is relevant to the meaning of the text, it is either illuminated with a textual footnote or included within parentheses in the text itself. For example, the footnote concerning the name "Eve" at Genesis 3:20 reads: "*Eve* sounds like a Hebrew term that means 'to give life.' " This wordplay in the Hebrew illuminates the meaning of the text, which goes on to say that Eve "would be the mother of all who live."

As WE SUBMIT this translation for publication, we recognize that any translation of the Scrip-tures is subject to limitations and imperfections. Anyone who has attempted to communi-cate the richness of God's Word into another language will realize it is impossible to make a perfect translation. Recognizing these limitations, we sought God's guidance and wisdom throughout this project. Now we pray that he will accept our efforts and use this translation for the benefit of the church and of all people.

We pray that the New Living Translation will overcome some of the barriers of history, cul-ture, and language that have kept people from reading and understanding God's Word. We hope that readers unfamiliar with the Bible will find the words clear and easy to understand and that readers well versed in the Scriptures will gain a fresh perspective. We pray that readers will gain insight and wisdom for living, but most of all that they will meet the God of the Bible and be forever changed by knowing him.

The Bible Translation Committee
October 2007

WHY THE
LIFE APPLICATION STUDY BIBLE
IS UNIQUE

Have you ever opened your Bible and asked the following:

- What does this passage really mean?
- How does it apply to my life?
- Why does some of the Bible seem irrelevant?
- What do these ancient cultures have to do with today?
- I love God; why can't I understand what he is saying to me through his word?
- What's going on in the lives of these Bible people?

Many Christians do not read the Bible regularly. Why? Because in the pressures of daily living they cannot find a connection between the timeless principles of Scripture and the ever-present problems of day-by-day living.

God urges us to apply his word (Isaiah 42:23; 1 Corinthians 10:11; 2 Thessalonians 3:4), but too often we stop at accumulating Bible knowledge. This is why the *Life Application Study Bible* was developed—to show how to put into practice what we have learned.

Applying God's word is a vital part of one's relationship with God; it is the evidence that we are obeying him. The difficulty in applying the Bible is not with the Bible itself, but with the reader's inability to bridge the gap between the past and present, the conceptual and practical. When we don't or can't do this, spiritual dryness, shallowness, and indifference are the results.

The words of Scripture itself cry out to us, "But don't just listen to God's word. You must do what it says. Otherwise, you are only fooling yourselves" (James 1:22). The *Life Application Study Bible* helps us to obey God's word. Developed by an interdenominational team of pastors, scholars, family counselors, and a national organization dedicated to promoting God's word and spreading the gospel, the *Life Application Study Bible* took many years to complete. All the work was reviewed by several renowned theologians under the directorship of Dr. Kenneth Kantzer.

The *Life Application Study Bible* does what a good resource Bible should: It helps you understand the context of a passage, gives important background and historical information, explains difficult words and phrases, and helps you see the interrelationship of Scripture. But it does much more. The *Life Application Study Bible* goes deeper into God's word, helping you discover the timeless truth being communicated, see the relevance for your life, and make a personal application. While some study Bibles attempt application, over 75 percent of this Bible is application oriented. The notes answer the questions "So what?" and "What does this passage mean to me, my family, my friends, my job, my neighborhood, my church, my country?"

Imagine reading a familiar passage of Scripture and gaining fresh insight, as if it were the first time you had ever read it. How much richer your life would be if you left each Bible reading with a new perspective and a small change for the better. A small change every day adds up to a changed life—and that is the very purpose of Scripture.

WHAT IS APPLICATION?

The best way to define application is to first determine what it is *not*. Application is *not* just accumulating knowledge. Accumulating knowledge helps us discover and understand facts and concepts, but it stops there. History is filled with philosophers who knew what the Bible said but failed to apply it to their lives, keeping them from believing and changing. Many think that understanding is the end goal of Bible study, but it is really only the beginning.

Application is *not* just illustration. Illustration only tells us how someone else handled a similar situation. While we may empathize with that person, we still have little direction for our personal situation.

Application is *not* just making a passage "relevant." Making the Bible relevant only helps us to see that the same lessons that were true in Bible times are true today; it does not show us how to apply them to the problems and pressures of our individual lives.

What, then, is application? Application begins by knowing and understanding God's word and its timeless truths. *But you cannot stop there*. If you do, God's word may not change your life, and it may become dull, difficult, tedious, and tiring. A good application focuses the truth of God's word, shows the reader what to do about what is being read, and motivates the reader to respond to what God is teaching. All three are essential to application.

Application is putting into practice what we already know (see Mark 4:24 and Hebrews 5:14) and answering the question "So what?" by confronting us with the right questions and motivating us to take action (see 1 John 2:5-6 and James 2:26). Application is deeply personal—unique for each individual. It makes a relevant truth a personal truth and involves developing a strategy and action plan to live your life in harmony with the Bible. It is the biblical "how to" of life.

You may ask, "How can your application notes be relevant to my life?" Each application note has three parts: (1) an *explanation*, which ties the note directly to the Scripture passage and sets up the truth that is being taught; (2) the *bridge*, which explains the timeless truth and makes it relevant for today; (3) the *application*, which shows you how to take the timeless truth and apply it to your personal situation. No note, by itself, can apply Scripture directly to your life. It can only teach, direct, lead, guide, inspire, recommend, and urge. It can give you the resources and direction you need to apply the Bible, but only you can take these resources and put them into practice.

A good note, therefore should not only give you knowledge and understanding but point you to application. Before you buy any kind of resource study Bible, you should evaluate the notes and ask the following questions: (1) Does the note contain enough information to help me understand the point of the Scripture passage? (2) Does the note assume I know more than I do? (3) Does the note avoid denominational bias? (4) Do the notes touch most of life's experiences? (5) Does the note help me apply God's word?

FEATURES OF THE
LIFE APPLICATION STUDY BIBLE

NOTES
In addition to providing the reader with many application notes, the *Life Application Study Bible* also offers several kinds of explanatory notes, which help the reader understand culture, history, context, difficult-to-understand passages, background, places, theological concepts, and the relationship of various passages in Scripture to other passages.

BOOK INTRODUCTIONS
Each book introduction is divided into several easy-to-find parts:

Timeline. A guide that puts the Bible book into its historical setting. It lists the key events and the dates when they occurred.

Vital Statistics. A list of straight facts about the book—those pieces of information you need to know at a glance.

Overview. A summary of the book with general lessons and applications that can be learned from the book as a whole.

Blueprint. The outline of the book. It is printed in easy-to-understand language and is designed for easy memorization. To the right of each main heading is a key lesson that is taught in that particular section.

Megathemes. A section that gives the main themes of the Bible book, explains their significance, and then tells you why they are still important for us today.

Map. If included, this shows the key places found in that book and retells the story of the book from a geographical point of view.

OUTLINE
The *Life Application Study Bible* has a new, custom-made outline that was designed specifically from an application point of view. Several unique features should be noted:

1. To avoid confusion and to aid memory work, the book outline has only three levels for headings. Main outline heads are marked with a capital letter. Subheads are marked by a number. Minor explanatory heads have no letter or number.

2. Each main outline head marked by a letter also has a brief paragraph below it summarizing the Bible text and offering a general application.

3. Parallel passages are listed where they apply.

PERSONALITY PROFILES
Among the unique features of this Bible are the profiles of key Bible people, including their strengths and weaknesses, greatest accomplishments and mistakes, and key lessons from their lives.

MAPS

The *Life Application Study Bible* has a thorough and comprehensive Bible atlas built right into the book. There are two kinds of maps: a book-introduction map, telling the story of the book, and thumbnail maps in the notes, plotting most geographic movements.

CHARTS AND DIAGRAMS

Many charts and diagrams are included to help the reader better visualize difficult concepts or relationships. Most charts not only present the needed information but show the significance of the information as well.

CROSS-REFERENCES

An updated, exhaustive cross-reference system in the margins of the Bible text helps the reader find related passages quickly.

TEXTUAL NOTES

Directly related to the text of the New Living Translation, the textual notes provide explanations on certain wording in the translation, alternate translations, and information about readings in the ancient manuscripts.

HIGHLIGHTED NOTES

In each Bible study lesson, you will be asked to read specific notes as part of your preparation. These notes have each been highlighted by a bullet (•) so that you can find them easily.

HEBREWS

CONSCIENTIOUS consumers shop for value, the best products for the money. Wise parents desire only the best for their children, nourishing their growing bodies, minds, and spirits. Individuals with integrity seek the best investment of time, talents, and treasures. In every area, to settle for less would be wasteful, foolish, and irresponsible. Yet it is a natural pull to move toward what is convenient and comfortable.

Judaism was not second-rate or easy. Divinely designed, it was the best religion, expressing true worship and devotion to God. The commandments, the rituals, and the prophets described God's promises and revealed the way to forgiveness and salvation. But Christ came, fulfilling the Law and the Prophets, conquering sin, shattering all barriers to God, freely providing eternal life.

This message was difficult for Jews to accept. Although they had sought the Messiah for centuries, they were entrenched in thinking and worshiping in traditional forms. Following Jesus seemed to repudiate their marvelous heritage and Scriptures. With caution and questions they listened to the gospel, but many rejected it and sought to eliminate this "heresy." Those who did accept Jesus as the Messiah often found themselves slipping back into familiar routines, trying to live a hybrid faith.

Hebrews is a masterful document written to Jews who were evaluating Jesus or struggling with this new faith. The message of Hebrews is that Jesus is better, Christianity is superior, Christ is supreme and completely sufficient for salvation.

Hebrews begins by emphasizing that the old (Judaism) and the new (Christianity) are both religions revealed by God (1:1–3). In the doctrinal section that follows (1:4—10:18), the writer shows how Jesus is superior to angels (1:4—2:18), superior to their leaders (3:1—4:13), and superior to their priests (4:14—7:28). Christianity surpasses Judaism because it has a better covenant (8:1–13), a better sanctuary (9:1–10), and a more sufficient sacrifice for sins (9:11—10:18).

Having established the superiority of Christianity, the writer moves on to the practical implications of following Christ. The readers are exhorted to hold on to their new faith, encourage each other, and look forward to Christ's return (10:19–25). They are warned about the consequences of rejecting Christ's sacrifice (10:26–31) and reminded of the rewards for faithfulness (10:32–39). Then the author explains how to live by faith, giving illustrations of the faithful men and women in Israel's history (11:1–40) and giving encouragement and exhortation for daily living (12:1–17). This section ends by comparing the old covenant with the new (12:18–29). The writer concludes with moral exhortations (13:1–17), a request for prayer (13:18, 19), and a benediction and greetings (13:20–25).

Whatever you are considering as the focus of life, Christ is better. He is the perfect revelation of God, the final and complete sacrifice for sin, the compassionate and understanding mediator, and the *only* way to eternal life. Read Hebrews and begin to see history and life from God's perspective. Then give yourself unreservedly and completely to Christ.

VITAL STATISTICS

PURPOSE:
To present the sufficiency and superiority of Christ

AUTHOR:
Paul, Luke, Barnabas, Apollos, Silas, Philip, Priscilla, and others have been suggested because the name of the author is not given in the biblical text itself. Whoever it was speaks of Timothy as "brother" (13:23).

ORIGINAL AUDIENCE:
Hebrew Christians (perhaps second-generation Christians, see 2:3) who may have been considering a return to Judaism, perhaps because of immaturity, stemming from a lack of understanding of biblical truths

DATE WRITTEN:
Probably before the destruction of the Temple in Jerusalem in A.D. 70 because the religious sacrifices and ceremonies are referred to in the book, but no mention is made of the Temple's destruction

SETTING:
These Jewish Christians were probably undergoing fierce persecution, socially and physically, both from Jews and from Romans. Christ had not returned to establish his Kingdom, and the people needed to be reassured that Christianity was true and that Jesus was indeed the Messiah.

KEY VERSE:
"The Son radiates God's own glory and expresses the very character of God, and he sustains everything by the mighty power of his command. When he had cleansed us from our sins, he sat down in the place of honor at the right hand of the majestic God in heaven" (1:3).

KEY PEOPLE:
Old Testament men and women of faith (chapter 11)

THE BLUEPRINT

A. THE SUPERIORITY OF CHRIST
   (1:1—10:18)
   1. Christ is greater than the angels
   2. Christ is greater than Moses
   3. Christ is greater than the Old
      Testament priesthood
   4. The new covenant is greater than
      the old

B. THE SUPERIORITY OF FAITH
   (10:19—13:25)

The superiority of Christ over everyone and everything is clearly demonstrated by the author. Christianity supersedes all other religions and can never be surpassed. Where can one find anything better than Christ? Living in Christ is having the best there is in life. All competing religions are deceptions or cheap imitations.

Jews who had become Christians in the first century were tempted to fall back into Judaism because of uncertainty, the security of custom, and persecution. Today believers are also tempted to fall back into legalism, fulfilling minimum religious requirements rather than pressing on in genuine faith. We must strive to live by faith each day.

MEGATHEMES

THEME	EXPLANATION	IMPORTANCE
Christ Is Superior	Hebrews reveals Jesus' true identity as God. Jesus is the ultimate authority. He is greater than any religion or any angel. He is superior to any Jewish leader (such as Abraham, Moses, or Joshua) and superior to any priest. He is the complete revelation of God.	Jesus alone can forgive our sin. He has secured our forgiveness and salvation by his death on the cross. We can find peace with God and real meaning for life by believing in Christ. We should not accept any alternative to or substitute for him.
High Priest	In the Old Testament, the high priest represented the Jews before God. Jesus Christ links us with God. There is no other way to reach God. Because Jesus Christ lived a sinless life, he is the perfect substitute to die for our sin. He is our perfect representative with God.	Jesus guarantees our access to God the Father. He intercedes for us so we can boldly come to the Father with our needs. When we are weak, we can come confidently to God for forgiveness and ask for his help.
Sacrifice	Christ's sacrifice was the ultimate fulfillment of all that the Old Testament sacrifices represented— God's forgiveness for sin. Because Christ is the perfect sacrifice for our sin, our sins are completely forgiven—past, present, and future.	Christ removed sin, which barred us from God's presence and fellowship. But we must accept his sacrifice for us. By believing in him, we are no longer guilty but cleansed and made whole. His sacrifice clears the way for us to have eternal life.
Maturity	Though we are saved from sin when we believe in Christ, we are given the task of going on and growing in our faith. Through our relationship with Christ, we can live blameless lives, be set aside for his special use, and develop maturity.	The process of maturing in our faith takes time. Daily commitment and service produce maturity. When we are mature in our faith, we are not easily swayed or shaken by temptations or worldly concerns.
Faith	Faith is confident trust in God's promises. God's greatest promise is that we can be saved through Jesus.	If we trust in Jesus Christ for our complete salvation, he will transform us completely. A life of obedience and complete trust is pleasing to God.
Endurance	Faith enables Christians to face trials. Genuine faith includes the commitment to stay true to God when we are under fire. Endurance builds character and leads to victory.	We can have victory in our trials if we don't give up or turn our back on Christ. Stay true to Christ and pray for endurance.

A. THE SUPERIORITY OF CHRIST (1:1—10:18)

The relationship of Christianity to Judaism was a critical issue in the early church. The author clears up confusion by carefully explaining how Christ is superior to angels, Moses, and high priests. The new covenant is shown to be far superior to the old. This can be a great encouragement to us and help us avoid drifting away from our faith in Christ.

1. Christ is greater than the angels

Jesus Christ Is God's Son

1:1
Num 12:6-8
1:2
Matt 21:38
John 1:3
1 Pet 1:20
1:3
Ps 110:1
John 14:9
2 Cor 4:4
Col 1:15

1 Long ago God spoke many times and in many ways to our ancestors through the prophets. ²And now in these final days, he has spoken to us through his Son. God promised everything to the Son as an inheritance, and through the Son he created the universe. ³ The Son radiates God's own glory and expresses the very character of God, and he sustains everything by the mighty power of his command. When he had cleansed us from our sins, he sat down in the place of honor at the right hand of the majestic God in heaven. ⁴This shows that the Son is far greater than the angels, just as the name God gave him is greater than their names.

CHRIST AND THE ANGELS

Hebrews passage	Old Testament passage	How Christ is superior to angels
1:5, 6	Psalm 2:7	Christ is called "Son" of God, a title never given to an angel.
1:7, 14	Psalm 104:4	Angels are important but are still only servants under God.
1:8, 9	Psalm 45:6	Christ's Kingdom is forever.
1:10	Psalm 102:25	Christ is the Creator of the world.
1:13	Psalm 110:1	Christ is given unique honor by God.

The writer of Hebrews quotes from the Old Testament repeatedly in demonstrating Christ's greatness in comparison to the angels. This audience of first-century Jewish Christians had developed an imbalanced belief in angels and their role. Christ's lordship is affirmed without disrespect to God's valued angelic messengers.

• 1:1 The book of Hebrews describes in detail how Jesus Christ not only fulfills the promises and prophecies of the Old Testament but is better than everything in the Jewish system of thought. The Jews accepted the Old Testament, but most of them rejected Jesus as the long-awaited Messiah. The recipients of this letter seem to have been Jewish Christians. They were well versed in Scripture, and they had professed faith in Christ. Whether through doubt, persecution, or false teaching, however, they may have been in danger of giving up their Christian faith and returning to Judaism.

The authorship of this book is uncertain. Several names have been suggested, including Luke, Barnabas, Apollos, Priscilla, and Paul. Most scholars do not believe that Paul was the author, because the writing style of Hebrews is quite different from that of his letters. In addition, Paul identified himself in his other letters and appealed to his authority as an apostle, whereas this writer of Hebrews, who never gives his or her name, appeals to eyewitnesses of Jesus' ministry for authority. Nevertheless, the author of Hebrews evidently knew Paul well. Hebrews was probably written by one of Paul's close associates who often heard him preach.

• 1:1, 2 God used many approaches to send his messages to people in Old Testament times. He spoke to Isaiah in visions (Isaiah 6), to Jacob in a dream (Genesis 28:10-22), and to Abraham and Moses personally (Genesis 18; Exodus 31:18). Jewish people familiar with these stories would not have found it hard to believe that God was still revealing his will, but it was astonishing for them to think that God had revealed *himself* by speaking through his Son, Jesus Christ. Jesus is the fulfillment and culmination of God's revelation through the centuries. When we know him, we have all we need to be saved from our sin and to have a perfect relationship with God.

1:2 Jesus was God's agent in creating the world: "For through him God created everything" (Colossians 1:16). As followers of Christ, we may give easy assent to this truth but deny it in practice. We may believe that Christ knows and controls the laws of heaven (pertaining to salvation and spiritual growth), but we may act each day as though our financial, family, or medical problems

are beyond his reach. If Jesus could create the universe, then no part of life is out of his control. Do not exclude Jesus' wisdom and the Bible's guidance in your complex problems of life. No expert, professor, doctor, lawyer, or financial adviser knows more about your ultimate security and well being than Jesus does. Go first to God for advice. Talk to him in prayer and listen to him in his Word. He can sustain you in times of stress. From that perspective you can evaluate all the other wisdom and help made available to you.

• 1:3 Not only is Jesus the exact representation of God, but he is God himself—the very God who spoke in Old Testament times. He is eternal; he worked with the Father in creating the world (John 1:3; Colossians 1:16). He is the full revelation of God. You can have no clearer view of God than by looking at Christ. Jesus Christ is the complete expression of God in a human body.

1:3 The book of Hebrews links God's saving power with his creative power. In other words, the power that brought the universe into being and that keeps it operating is the very power that cleanses our sins. How mistaken we would be to ever think that God couldn't forgive us. No sin is too big for the Ruler of the universe to handle. He can and will forgive us when we come to him through his Son. That Jesus *sat down* means that the work was complete. Christ's sacrifice was final.

• 1:4 The "far greater" name that was given to Jesus is "Son." This name given to him by his Father is greater than the names and titles of the angels.

• 1:4ff False teachers in many of the early churches taught that God could be approached only through angels. Instead of worshiping God directly, followers of these heretics revered angels. Hebrews clearly denounces such teaching as false. Some thought of Jesus as the highest angel of God. But Jesus is not a superior angel, and in any case, angels are not to be worshiped (see Colossians 2:18; Revelation 19:1-10). We should not regard any intermediaries or authorities as greater than Christ. Jesus is God. He alone deserves our worship.

The Son Is Greater Than the Angels

5For God never said to any angel what he said to Jesus:

> "You are my Son.
> Today I have become your Father.*"

God also said,

> "I will be his Father,
> and he will be my Son."*

6And when he brought his supreme* Son into the world, God said,*

> "Let all of God's angels worship him."*

7Regarding the angels, he says,

> "He sends his angels like the winds,
> his servants like flames of fire."*

8But to the Son he says,

> "Your throne, O God, endures forever and ever.
> You rule with a scepter of justice.
> 9 You love justice and hate evil.
> Therefore, O God, your God has anointed you,
> pouring out the oil of joy on you more than on anyone else."*

10He also says to the Son,

> "In the beginning, Lord, you laid the foundation of the earth
> and made the heavens with your hands.
> 11 They will perish, but you remain forever.
> They will wear out like old clothing.
> 12 You will fold them up like a cloak
> and discard them like old clothing.
> But you are always the same;
> you will live forever."*

13And God never said to any of the angels,

> "Sit in the place of honor at my right hand
> until I humble your enemies,
> making them a footstool under your feet."*

14Therefore, angels are only servants—spirits sent to care for people who will inherit salvation.

1:5
†Ps 2:7
†2 Sam 7:14

1:6
†Deut 32:43
†Ps 8:4

1:7
†Pss 8:5; 104:4

1:8-9
†Ps 45:6-7

1:10-12
†Ps 102:25-27

1:13
Ps 110:1
Matt 22:44

1:14
Pss 34:7; 91:11

1:5a Or *Today I reveal you as my Son.* Ps 2:7.   **1:5b** 2 Sam 7:14.   **1:6a** Or *firstborn.*   **1:6b** Or *when he again brings his supreme Son* [or *firstborn Son*] *into the world, God will say.*   **1:6c** Deut 32:43.   **1:7** Ps 104:4 (Greek version).   **1:8-9** Ps 45:6-7.   **1:10-12** Ps 102:25-27.   **1:13** Ps 110:1.

1:5, 6 Jesus is God's honored, firstborn Son. In Jewish families the firstborn son held the place of highest privilege and responsibility. The Jewish Christians reading this message would understand that as God's firstborn, Jesus was superior to any created being.

1:10-12 The author of Hebrews quotes Psalm 102:25-27. In the quotation, he regards God as the speaker and applies the words to the Son, Jesus. The earth and the heavens folded up like a cloak reveals that the earth is not permanent or indestructible (a position held by many Greek and Roman philosophies). Jesus' authority is established over all of creation, so we dare not treat any created object or earthly resource as more important than he is. When we spend more time on ourselves than on serving Christ, we treat ourselves (his creation) as being more important than our Creator. When we regard our finances, rather than our faith in Christ, as the basis for security, we give higher status to an earthly resource than we do to God. Rather than trusting in changeable and temporary resources, trust in God, who is eternal.

• **1:11, 12** Because the readers of Hebrews (Jewish Christians) had experienced the rejection of their fellow Jews, they often felt isolated. Many were tempted to exchange the changeless Christ for their familiar old faith. The writer of Hebrews warned them not to do this: Christ is our *only* security in a changing world. Whatever may happen in this world, Christ remains forever changeless. If we trust him, we are absolutely secure, because we stand on the firmest foundation in the universe—Jesus Christ. A famous hymn captures this truth: "On Christ the solid rock I stand, all other ground is sinking sand."

1:12 What does it mean that Christ is changeless ("you are always the same")? It means that Christ's character will never change. He persistently shows his love to us. He is always fair, just, and merciful to us who are so undeserving. Be thankful that Christ is changeless; he will always help you when you need it and offer forgiveness when you fall.

• **1:14** Angels are God's messengers, spiritual beings created by God and under his authority (Colossians 1:16). They have several functions: serving believers (1:14), protecting the helpless (Matthew 18:10), proclaiming God's messages (Revelation 14:6-12), and executing God's judgment (Acts 12:1-23; Revelation 20:1-3).

A Warning against Drifting Away

2 So we must listen very carefully to the truth we have heard, or we may drift away from it. ²For the message God delivered through angels has always stood firm, and every violation of the law and every act of disobedience was punished. ³So what makes us think we can escape if we ignore this great salvation that was first announced by the Lord Jesus himself and then delivered to us by those who heard him speak? ⁴And God confirmed the message by giving signs and wonders and various miracles and gifts of the Holy Spirit whenever he chose.

2:2
Deut 33:2
Acts 7:38, 53
Gal 3:19
2:3
Heb 1:2; 10:29
2:4
Mark 16:20

Jesus, the Man

⁵And furthermore, it is not angels who will control the future world we are talking about. ⁶For in one place the Scriptures say,

2:6-8
Ps 8:4-6

> "What are mere mortals that you should think about them,
>   or a son of man* that you should care for him?
> ⁷ Yet you made them only a little lower than the angels
>   and crowned them with glory and honor.*
> ⁸ You gave them authority over all things."*

2:8
1 Cor 15:27

Now when it says "all things," it means nothing is left out. But we have not yet seen all things put under their authority. ⁹What we do see is Jesus, who was given a position "a little lower than the angels"; and because he suffered death for us, he is now "crowned with glory and

2:9
Phil 2:6-9

2:6 Or *the Son of Man.*   **2:7** Some manuscripts add *You gave them charge of everything you made.*
2:6-8 Ps 8:4-6 (Greek version).

LESSONS FROM CHRIST'S HUMANITY

Christ is the perfect human leader . . . . and he wants to lead you

model . . . . and he is worth imitating

sacrifice. . . . . . . and he died for you

conqueror . . . . . and he conquered death to give you eternal life

High Priest . . . . and he is merciful, loving, and understanding

God, in Christ, became a living, breathing human being. Hebrews points out many reasons why this is so important.

2:1-3 The author called his readers to pay attention to the truth they had heard so that they wouldn't drift away into false teachings. Paying careful attention is hard work. It involves focusing our mind, body, and senses. Listening to Christ means not merely hearing but also obeying (see James 1:22-25). We must listen carefully and be ready to carry out his instructions.

2:1 These early believers were in danger of falling away from following Jesus. They had heard the words of the gospel, but those words had not sunk in. People raised in believing families and churches risk the same danger today. They hear the words and more or less agree, but mental assent to Christ's leadership is insufficient to be Christ's disciple. Are you a Sunday school teacher, a small group leader, or a club leader? Don't assume that people who comply and conform are truly committed to Christ. Get to know each person who attends your group and challenge each with the truth and implications of commitment to Christ. Don't surrender anyone to casual belief.

2:2, 3 "The message God delivered through angels" refers to the teaching that angels, as messengers for God, had brought the law to Moses (see Galatians 3:19). A central theme of Hebrews is that Christ is infinitely greater than all other proposed ways to God. The author was saying that the faith of his Jewish readers was good, but faith must point to Christ. Just as Christ is greater than angels, so Christ's message is more important than theirs. No one will escape God's punishment if he or she is indifferent to the salvation offered by Christ.

2:3 Eyewitnesses to Jesus' ministry had handed down his teachings to the readers of this book. These readers were second-generation believers who had not seen Christ in the flesh. They are like us; we have not seen Jesus personally. We base our belief in Jesus on the eyewitness accounts recorded in the Bible. See John 20:29 for Jesus' encouragement to those who believe without out ever having seen him.

2:4 "God confirmed the message" continues the thought from 2:3. Those who had heard Jesus speak and then had passed on his words also had the truth of their words confirmed by "signs and wonders and various miracles and gifts of the Holy Spirit." In the book of Acts, miracles and gifts of the Spirit authenticated the Good News wherever it was preached (see Acts 9:31-42; 14:1-20). Paul, who discussed spiritual gifts in Romans 12, 1 Corinthians 12–14, and Ephesians 4, taught that their purpose is to build up the church, making it strong and mature. When we see the gifts of the Spirit in an individual or congregation, we know that God is truly present. As we receive God's gifts, we should thank him for them and put them to use in the church.

2:8, 9 God put Jesus in charge of everything, and Jesus revealed himself to us. We do not yet see Jesus reigning on earth, but we can picture him in his heavenly glory. When you are confused by present events and anxious about the future, remember Jesus' true position and authority. He is Lord of all, and one day he will rule on earth as he does now in heaven. This truth can give stability to your decisions day by day.

● **2:9, 10** God's grace to us led Christ to his death. Jesus did not come into the world to gain status or political power, but to suffer and die so that we could have eternal life ("bring many children into glory"). If it is difficult for us to identify with Christ's servant attitude, perhaps we need to evaluate our own motives. Are we more interested in power or participation, domination or service, getting or giving?

honor." Yes, by God's grace, Jesus tasted death for everyone. [10]God, for whom and through whom everything was made, chose to bring many children into glory. And it was only right that he should make Jesus, through his suffering, a perfect leader, fit to bring them into their salvation.

2:10
Luke 13:32; 24:46
Rom 11:36
Heb 5:9

[11]So now Jesus and the ones he makes holy have the same Father. That is why Jesus is not ashamed to call them his brothers and sisters.* [12]For he said to God,

2:11
Matt 28:10
John 20:17
Rom 8:29
Heb 10:10; 13:12

"I will proclaim your name to my brothers and sisters.
    I will praise you among your assembled people."*

2:12
†Ps 22:22

[13]He also said,

2:13
†Isa 8:17-18
John 17:11-12

"I will put my trust in him,"
    that is, "I and the children God has given me."*

[14]Because God's children are human beings—made of flesh and blood—the Son also became flesh and blood. For only as a human being could he die, and only by dying could he break the power of the devil, who had* the power of death. [15]Only in this way could he set free all who have lived their lives as slaves to the fear of dying.

2:14
John 1:14
Rom 8:3
1 Cor 15:54-57
2 Tim 1:10
1 Jn 3:8

[16]We also know that the Son did not come to help angels; he came to help the descendants of Abraham. [17]Therefore, it was necessary for him to be made in every respect like us, his brothers and sisters,* so that he could be our merciful and faithful High Priest before God. Then he could offer a sacrifice that would take away the sins of the people. [18]Since he himself has gone through suffering and testing, he is able to help us when we are being tested.

2:17
Phil 2:7
Heb 3:1; 4:15; 5:1
1 Jn 2:2; 4:10

2:18
Heb 4:15; 5:2

2. Christ is greater than Moses

3 And so, dear brothers and sisters who belong to God and* are partners with those called to heaven, think carefully about this Jesus whom we declare to be God's messenger* and High Priest. [2]For he was faithful to God, who appointed him, just as Moses served faithfully when he was entrusted with God's entire* house.

3:1
Heb 2:17; 4:14

3:2
Num 12:7-8

2:11 Greek *brothers;* also in 2:12.   **2:12** Ps 22:22.   **2:13** Isa 8:17-18.   **2:14** Or *has.*   **2:17** Greek *like the brothers.*
3:1a Greek *And so, holy brothers who.*   **3:1b** Greek *God's apostle.*   **3:2** Some manuscripts do not include *entire.*

2:10 How was Jesus made a perfect leader through suffering? Jesus' suffering made him a perfect leader, or pioneer, of our salvation (see the notes on 5:8 and 5:9). Jesus did not need to suffer for his own salvation, because he was God in human form. His perfect obedience (which led him down the road of suffering) demonstrates that he was the complete sacrifice for us. Through suffering, Jesus completed the work necessary for our own salvation. Our suffering can make us more sensitive servants of God. People who have known pain are able to reach out with compassion to others who hurt. If you have suffered, ask God how your experience can be used to help others.

• **2:11-13** We who have been set apart for God's service, cleansed, and made holy (sanctified) by Jesus now have the same Father he has, so he has made us his brothers and sisters. Various psalms look forward to Christ and his work in the world. Here the writer quotes a portion of Psalm 22, a messianic psalm. Because God has adopted all believers as his children, Jesus calls them his brothers and sisters.

2:14, 15 Jesus had to become human so that he could die and rise again in order to destroy the devil's power over death (Romans 6:5-11). Only then could Christ deliver those who had lived in constant fear of death and free them to live for him. When we belong to God, we need not fear death, because we know that death is only the doorway into eternal life (1 Corinthians 15).

• **2:14, 15** Christ's death and resurrection set us free from the fear of death because death has been defeated. Every person must die, but death is not the end; instead, it is the doorway to a new life. All who dread death should have the opportunity to know the hope that Christ's victory brings. How can you share this truth with those close to you?

• **2:16, 17** In the Old Testament, the high priest was the mediator between God and his people. His job was to regularly offer animal sacrifices according to the law and to intercede with God for

forgiveness of the people's sins. Jesus Christ is now our High Priest. He came to earth as a human being; therefore, he understands our weaknesses and shows mercy to us. He has *once and for all* paid the penalty for our sins by his own sacrificial death (atonement), and he can be depended on to restore our broken relationship with God. We are released from sin's domination over us when we commit ourselves fully to Christ, trusting completely in what he has done for us (see the note on 4:14 for more about Jesus as the great High Priest).

• **2:18** Knowing that Christ suffered pain and faced temptation helps us face our trials. Jesus understands our struggles because he faced them as a human being. We can trust Christ to help us survive suffering and overcome temptation. When you face trials, go to Jesus for strength and patience. He understands your needs and is able to help (see 4:14-16).

3:1 This verse would have been especially meaningful to Jewish Christians. For Jews, the highest human authority was the high priest. For Christians, the highest human authorities were God's messengers, the apostles. Jesus, God's messenger and High Priest, is the ultimate authority in the church.

3:1 The writer says to "think carefully about this Jesus," to fix our minds, ponder carefully, and focus on the true significance of Jesus. How much do we do that? In our age of sound bites, fast food, and quick-fix solutions, very few people take time to think about anything or anyone. In Jesus we have one to whom we should listen (God's messenger), through whom we come to the Father (High Priest), and to whom we give obedience (he is entrusted with God's entire house). When you think about the significance and superiority of Jesus, how does it affect your life today? Your decisions? Your actions?

3:2, 3 To the Jewish people, Moses was a great hero; he had led their ancestors, the Israelites, from Egyptian bondage to the border of the Promised Land. He also had written the first five

3:3
2 Cor 3:7-11

³But Jesus deserves far more glory than Moses, just as a person who builds a house deserves more praise than the house itself. ⁴For every house has a builder, but the one who built everything is God.

3:5
Exod 14:31
Num 12:7

⁵Moses was certainly faithful in God's house as a servant. His work was an illustration of the truths God would reveal later. ⁶But Christ, as the Son, is in charge of God's entire house.

3:6
Eph 2:19-22
1 Tim 3:15
1 Pet 2:5

And we are God's house, if we keep our courage and remain confident in our hope in Christ.*

3:7-11
†Ps 95:7-11

⁷That is why the Holy Spirit says,

3:8
Exod 17:7

"Today when you hear his voice,
  8   don't harden your hearts
       as Israel did when they rebelled,
       when they tested me in the wilderness.
   9 There your ancestors tested and tried my patience,
       even though they saw my miracles for forty years.
  10 So I was angry with them, and I said,
       'Their hearts always turn away from me.
       They refuse to do what I tell them.'

3:11
Num 14:21-23

  11 So in my anger I took an oath:
       'They will never enter my place of rest.'"*

3:13
Eph 4:22

¹²Be careful then, dear brothers and sisters.* Make sure that your own hearts are not evil and unbelieving, turning you away from the living God. ¹³You must warn each other every day, while it is still "today," so that none of you will be deceived by sin and hardened against God.

3:14
Heb 3:6

¹⁴For if we are faithful to the end, trusting God just as firmly as when we first believed, we will share in all that belongs to Christ. ¹⁵Remember what it says:

3:15
†Ps 95:7-8

"Today when you hear his voice,
   don't harden your hearts
   as Israel did when they rebelled."*

3:6 Some manuscripts add *faithful to the end.*   **3:7-11** Ps 95:7-11.   **3:12** Greek *brothers.*   **3:15** Ps 95:7-8.

---

books of the Old Testament, and he was the prophet through whom God had given the law; therefore, Moses was the greatest prophet in the Scriptures. But Jesus is worthy of greater honor as the central figure of faith than Moses, who was merely a human servant. Jesus is more than human; he is God himself (1:3). As Moses led the people of Israel out of Egyptian bondage, so Christ leads us out of sin's slavery. Why settle for Moses, the author of Hebrews asks, when you can have Jesus Christ, who appointed Moses?

3:5 Moses was faithful to God's calling not only to deliver Israel but also to prepare the way for the Messiah ("his work was an illustration of the truths God would reveal later"). All the Old Testament believers also served to prepare the way. Thus, knowing the Old Testament is the best foundation for understanding the New Testament. In reading the Old Testament, we see (1) how God used people to accomplish his purposes, (2) how God used events and personalities to illustrate important truths, (3) how, through prophets, God announced the Messiah, and (4) how, through the system of sacrifices, God prepared people to understand the Messiah's work. If you include the Old Testament in your regular Bible reading, the New Testament will grow clearer and more meaningful to you.

3:6 Because Christ lives in us as believers, we can remain courageous and hopeful to the end. We are not saved by being steadfast and firm in our faith, but our courage and hope do reveal that our faith is real. Without this enduring faithfulness, we could easily be blown away by the winds of temptation, false teaching, or persecution (see also 3:14).

• **3:7-15** This passage refers to the Israelites who had hardened their hearts in the wilderness. A hardened heart is as useless as a hardened lump of clay or a hardened loaf of bread. Nothing can restore it and make it useful. The writer of Psalm 95 warns against hardening our hearts as Israel did in the wilderness by continuing to resist God's will (Exodus 17:7; Numbers 13; 14; 20). The people

were so convinced that God couldn't deliver them that they simply lost their faith in him. People with hardened hearts are so stubbornly set in their ways that they cannot turn to God. This does not happen suddenly or all at once; it is the result of a series of choices to disregard God's will. Let people know that those who resist God long enough, God will toss aside like hardened bread, useless and worthless.

• **3:11** God's *rest* has several meanings in Scripture: (1) the seventh day of creation and the weekly Sabbath commemorating it (Genesis 2:2; Hebrews 4:4-9); (2) the Promised Land of Canaan (Deuteronomy 12:8-12; Psalm 95); (3) peace with God now because of our relationship with Christ through faith (Matthew 11:28; Hebrews 4:1, 3, 8-11); and (4) our future eternal life with Christ (Hebrews 4:8-11). All of these meanings were probably familiar to the Jewish Christian readers of Hebrews. We can apply the verses as a warning about God's anger in the face of human rebellion against his Kingdom. By rejecting God's provision (Christ) and not enduring in our faith, we miss the opportunity for spiritual rest.

• **3:12-14** Our hearts turn away from the living God when we stubbornly refuse to believe him. If we persist in our unbelief, God will eventually leave us alone in our sin. But God can give us new hearts, new desires, and new spirits (Ezekiel 36:22-27). To prevent having an unbelieving heart, stay in fellowship with other believers, talk daily about your mutual faith, be aware of the deceitfulness of sin (it attracts but also destroys), and encourage each other with love and concern.

• **3:15-19** The Israelites failed to enter the Promised Land because they did not believe in God's protection, and they did not believe that God would help them conquer the giants in the land (see Numbers 14–15). So God sent them into the wilderness to wander for 40 years. This was an unhappy alternative to the wonderful gift he had planned for them. Lack of trust in God always prevents us from receiving his best.

¹⁶And who was it who rebelled against God, even though they heard his voice? Wasn't it the people Moses led out of Egypt? ¹⁷And who made God angry for forty years? Wasn't it the people who sinned, whose corpses lay in the wilderness? ¹⁸And to whom was God speaking when he took an oath that they would never enter his rest? Wasn't it the people who disobeyed him? ¹⁹So we see that because of their unbelief they were not able to enter his rest.

3:16-18
Num 14:1-35
3:17
Num 14:29
1 Cor 10:5
3:18
Num 14:22-23

Promised Rest for God's People

4 God's promise of entering his rest still stands, so we ought to tremble with fear that some of you might fail to experience it. ²For this good news—that God has prepared this rest—has been announced to us just as it was to them. But it did them no good because they didn't share the faith of those who listened to God.* ³For only we who believe can enter his rest. As for the others, God said,

4:2
1 Thes 2:13
4:3
†Ps 95:11

"In my anger I took an oath:
    'They will never enter my place of rest,'"*

even though this rest has been ready since he made the world. ⁴We know it is ready because of the place in the Scriptures where it mentions the seventh day: "On the seventh day God rested from all his work."* ⁵But in the other passage God said, "They will never enter my place of rest."*

4:4
†Gen 2:2
4:5
†Ps 95:11
4:6
Heb 3:18
4:7
†Ps 95:7-8

⁶So God's rest is there for people to enter, but those who first heard this good news failed to enter because they disobeyed God. ⁷So God set another time for entering his rest, and that time is today. God announced this through David much later in the words already quoted:

"Today when you hear his voice,
    don't harden your hearts."*

⁸Now if Joshua had succeeded in giving them this rest, God would not have spoken about another day of rest still to come. ⁹So there is a special rest* still waiting for the people of God. ¹⁰For all who have entered into God's rest have rested from their labors, just as God did after creating the world. ¹¹So let us do our best to enter that rest. But if we disobey God, as the people of Israel did, we will fall.

4:8
Josh 22:4
4:10
Gen 2:2
Rev 14:13

4:2 Some manuscripts read *they didn't combine what they heard with faith.*   **4:3** Ps 95:11.   **4:4** Gen 2:2.
4:5 Ps 95:11.   **4:7** Ps 95:7-8.   **4:9** Or *a Sabbath rest.*

• **4:1-3** Some of the Jewish Christians who received this letter may have been on the verge of turning back from their promised rest in Christ, just as the people in Moses' day had turned back from the Promised Land. In both cases, the difficulties of the present moment overshadowed the reality of God's promise, and the people doubted that God would fulfill his promises. When we trust our own efforts instead of Christ's power, we, too, are in danger of turning back. Our own efforts are never adequate; only Christ can see us through.

4:2 The Israelites of Moses' day illustrate a problem facing many who fill our churches today. They know a great deal about Christ, but they do not know him personally—they don't combine their knowledge with faith. Let the Good News about Christ benefit your life. Believe in him and then act on what you know. Trust in Christ and do what he says.

• **4:4** God rested on the seventh day, not because he was tired, but to indicate the completion of creation. The world was perfect, and God was well satisfied with it. This rest is a foretaste of our eternal joy when creation will be renewed and restored, every mark of sin will be removed, and the world will be made perfect again. Our Sabbath-rest in Christ begins when we trust him to complete his good and perfect work in us (see the note on 3:11).

• **4:6, 7** God had given the Israelites the opportunity to enter Canaan, but they disobeyed and failed to enter (Numbers 13–14). Now God offers us the opportunity to enter his ultimate place of rest—he invites us to come to Christ. To enter his rest, you must believe that God has this relationship in mind for you; you must stop trying to create it; you must trust in Christ for it; and you must determine to obey him. *Today* is the best time to find peace with God. Tomorrow may be too late.

• **4:8-11** God wants us to enter his rest. For the Israelites of Moses' time, this rest was the earthly rest to be found in the Promised Land. For Christians, it is peace with God now and eternal life on a new earth later. We do not need to wait for the next life to enjoy God's rest and peace; we may have it daily now! Our daily rest in the Lord will not end with death but will become an eternal rest in the place that Christ is preparing for us (John 14:1-4).

4:10 Busy people often work especially hard the week before vacation, tying up loose ends so they can relax. Students usually have their final exams right before semester breaks. When we know a rest is coming, we put extra effort into finishing our work.

Healthy Christians love the work God has given them, doing it with passion and gusto, putting all their strength and care into it. But Christians love God's promise of heaven's rest even more and look forward to God's rest with great joy. Today, renew your effort to work hard for God. Rest is coming. Relish the thought.

• **4:11** If Jesus has provided for our rest through faith, why must we "do our best to enter that rest"? This is not the struggle of doing good in order to obtain salvation, nor is it a mystical struggle to overcome selfishness. It refers to making every effort to appreciate and benefit from what God has already provided. Salvation is not to be taken for granted; to appropriate the gift God offers requires decision and commitment.

4:12
Isa 49:2
Jer 23:29
1 Cor 14:24-25
Eph 6:17
1 Pet 1:23

4:13
2 Chr 16:9
Ps 33:13-15

4:14
Heb 2:17; 3:1

4:15
2 Cor 5:21
Heb 2:17-18

4:16
Heb 7:19

5:1
Heb 2:17; 7:27; 8:3

5:2
Heb 2:17; 4:15

5:3
Lev 9:7; 16:6
Heb 7:27; 9:7

5:4
Exod 28:1

5:5
Acts 13:33

¹²For the word of God is alive and powerful. It is sharper than the sharpest two-edged sword, cutting between soul and spirit, between joint and marrow. It exposes our innermost thoughts and desires. ¹³Nothing in all creation is hidden from God. Everything is naked and exposed before his eyes, and he is the one to whom we are accountable.

3. Christ is greater than the Old Testament priesthood
Christ Is Our High Priest

¹⁴So then, since we have a great High Priest who has entered heaven, Jesus the Son of God, let us hold firmly to what we believe. ¹⁵This High Priest of ours understands our weaknesses, for he faced all of the same testings we do, yet he did not sin. ¹⁶So let us come boldly to the throne of our gracious God. There we will receive his mercy, and we will find grace to help us when we need it most.

5 Every high priest is a man chosen to represent other people in their dealings with God. He presents their gifts to God and offers sacrifices for their sins. ²And he is able to deal gently with ignorant and wayward people because he himself is subject to the same weaknesses. ³That is why he must offer sacrifices for his own sins as well as theirs.

⁴And no one can become a high priest simply because he wants such an honor. He must be called by God for this work, just as Aaron was. ⁵That is why Christ did not honor himself by assuming he could become High Priest. No, he was chosen by God, who said to him,

---

THE CHOICES OF MATURITY

Mature Choices	*Versus*	*Immature Choices*
Teaching others	rather than. . . .	just being taught
Developing depth of understanding . . .	rather than. . . .	struggling with the basics
Self-evaluation	rather than. . . .	self-criticism
Seeking unity	rather than. . . .	promoting disunity
Desiring spiritual challenges	rather than. . . .	desiring entertainment
Careful study and observation	rather than. . . .	opinions and halfhearted efforts
Active faith	rather than. . . .	cautious apathy and doubt
Confidence.	rather than. . . .	fear
Feelings and experiences evaluated in the light of God's Word.	rather than. . . .	experiences evaluated according to feelings

One way to evaluate spiritual maturity is by looking at the choices we make. The writer of Hebrews notes many of the ways these choices change with personal growth.

• **4:12** The Word of God is not simply a collection of words from God, a vehicle for communicating ideas; it is living, life-changing, and dynamic as it works in us. With the incisiveness of a surgeon's knife, God's Word reveals who we are and what we are not. It penetrates the core of our moral and spiritual life. It discerns what is within us, both good and evil. The demands of God's Word require decisions. We must not only listen to the Word; we must also let it shape our lives.

• **4:13** Nothing can be hidden from God. He knows about everyone everywhere, and everything about us is wide open to his all-seeing eyes. God sees all we do and knows all we think. Even when we are unaware of his presence, he is there. When we try to hide from him, he sees us. We can have no secrets from God. It is comforting to realize that although God knows us intimately, he still loves us.

4:14 Christ is superior to the priests, and his priesthood is superior to their priesthood. To the Jews, the high priest was the highest religious authority in the land. He alone entered the Most Holy Place in the Temple once a year to make atonement for the sins of the whole nation (Leviticus 16). Like the high priest, Jesus mediates between God and us. As humanity's representative, he intercedes for us before God. As God's representative, he assures us of God's forgiveness. Jesus has more authority than the Jewish high priests because he is truly God and truly man. Unlike the high priest, who could go before God only once a year, Christ is

always at God's right hand, interceding for us. He is always available to hear us when we pray.

4:15 Jesus is like us because he experienced a full range of temptations throughout his life as a human being. We can be comforted knowing that Jesus faced temptation—he can sympathize with us. We can be encouraged knowing that Jesus faced temptation without giving in to sin. He shows us that we do not have to sin when facing the seductive lure of temptation. Jesus is the only perfect human being who has ever lived.

4:16 Prayer is our approach to God, and we are to come "boldly." Some Christians approach God meekly with heads hung low, afraid to ask him to meet their needs. Others pray flippantly, giving little thought to what they say. Come with reverence because he is your King. But also come with bold assurance because he is your Friend and Counselor.

5:4-6 This chapter stresses both Christ's divine appointment and his humanity. The writer uses two Old Testament verses to show Christ's divine appointment: Psalms 2:7 and 110:4. At the time this book was written, the Romans selected the high priest in Jerusalem. In the Old Testament, however, God chose Aaron, and only Aaron's descendants could be high priests. Christ, like Aaron, was chosen and called by God.

"You are my Son.

Today I have become your Father.*"

[6] And in another passage God said to him,

"You are a priest forever in the order of Melchizedek."*

[7] While Jesus was here on earth, he offered prayers and pleadings, with a loud cry and tears, to the one who could rescue him from death. And God heard his prayers because of his deep reverence for God. [8] Even though Jesus was God's Son, he learned obedience from the things he suffered. [9] In this way, God qualified him as a perfect High Priest, and he became the source of eternal salvation for all those who obey him. [10] And God designated him to be a High Priest in the order of Melchizedek.

A Call to Spiritual Growth

[11] There is much more we would like to say about this, but it is difficult to explain, especially since you are spiritually dull and don't seem to listen. [12] You have been believers so long now that you ought to be teaching others. Instead, you need someone to teach you again the basic things about God's word.* You are like babies who need milk and cannot eat solid food. [13] For someone who lives on milk is still an infant and doesn't know how to do what is right. [14] Solid food is for those who are mature, who through training have the skill to recognize the difference between right and wrong.

6 So let us stop going over the basic teachings about Christ again and again. Let us go on instead and become mature in our understanding. Surely we don't need to start again with the fundamental importance of repenting from evil deeds* and placing our faith in God. [2] You don't need further instruction about baptisms, the laying on of hands, the resurrection of the dead, and eternal judgment. [3] And so, God willing, we will move forward to further understanding.

5:6
†Ps 110:4

5:7
Matt 26:38-46
Mark 14:32-42
Luke 22:39-46

5:8
Phil 2:8
Heb 1:2

5:10
Ps 110:4
Heb 5:6

5:12
1 Cor 3:2
1 Pet 2:2

5:13
1 Cor 14:20
Eph 4:14

5:14
Rom 16:19
1 Cor 2:6

6:1
Phil 3:12-14
Heb 5:12; 9:14

6:2
Acts 2:4; 6:6;
17:18, 32

5:5 Or *Today I reveal you as my Son.* Ps 2:7.   **5:6** Ps 110:4.   **5:12** Or *about the oracles of God.*   **6:1** Greek *from dead works.*

5:6 Melchizedek was a priest of Salem (now called Jerusalem). His Profile is found in Genesis 15, p. 29. Melchizedek's position is explained in Hebrews 7.

5:7 Jesus was in great agony as he prepared to face death (Luke 22:41-44). Although Jesus cried out to God, asking to be delivered, he was prepared to suffer humiliation, separation from his Father, and death in order to do God's will. At times we will undergo trials, not because we want to suffer, but because we want to obey God. Let Jesus' obedience sustain and encourage you in times of trial. You will be able to face anything if you know that Jesus Christ is with you.

5:7 Have you ever felt that God didn't hear your prayers? Be sure you are praying with reverent submission, willing to do what God wants. God responds to his obedient children.

5:8 Jesus' human life was not a script that he passively followed. It was a life that he chose freely (John 10:17, 18). It was a continuous process of making the will of God the Father his own. Jesus chose to obey, even though obedience led to suffering and death. Because Jesus obeyed perfectly, even under great trial, he can help us obey, no matter how difficult obedience seems to be.

5:9 Christ was always morally perfect. By obeying, he demonstrated his perfection to us, not to God or to himself. In the Bible, *perfect* usually means completeness or maturity. By sharing our experience of suffering, Christ shared our human experience completely. He is now able to offer eternal salvation to those who obey him. See Philippians 2:5-11 for Christ's attitude as he took on human form.

5:9 The "eternal salvation" we have been offered means the elimination of a verdict on our sin, the setting aside of judgment, and the award of undeserved membership in God's family. It is a change in destiny, an awakening of hope, an overcoming of death. Salvation turns a person toward heaven and inaugurates a life of discipleship with the living Christ. It is God's vote for you, God's invitation to you, God's energy invested in you. Salvation is

the reason you can smile in the morning and rest in the evening. God loves you, and you belong to him.

• **5:12, 13** These Jewish Christians were immature. Some of them should have been teaching others, but they had not even applied the basics to their own lives. They were reluctant to move beyond age-old traditions, established doctrines, and discussion of the basics. They wouldn't be able to understand the high-priestly role of Christ unless they moved out of their comfortable position, cut some of their Jewish ties, and stopped trying to blend in with their culture. Commitment to Christ moves people out of their comfort zones.

• **5:12-14** In order to grow from infant Christians to mature Christians, we must learn discernment. We must train our conscience, our senses, our mind, and our body to distinguish good from evil. Can you recognize temptation before it traps you? Can you tell the difference between a correct use of Scripture and a mistaken one?

• **5:14** Our capacity to feast on deeper knowledge of God ("solid food") is determined by our spiritual growth. Too often we want God's banquet before we are spiritually capable of digesting it. As you grow in the Lord and put into practice what you have learned, your capacity to understand will also grow.

• **6:1, 2** Certain basic teachings are essential for all believers to understand. Those basics include the importance of faith, the foolishness of trying to be saved by good deeds, the meaning of baptism and spiritual gifts, and the facts of resurrection and eternal life. To go on to maturity in our understanding, we need to move beyond (but not away from) the basic teachings to a more complete understanding of the faith. And this is what the author intends for his readers to do (6:3). Mature Christians should be teaching new Christians the basics. Then, acting on what they know, the mature will learn even more from God's Word.

6:3 These Christians needed to move beyond the basics of their faith to an understanding of Christ as the perfect High

Not ~~Natonal~~ RECEIVED   *Pg 145 / 40*

6:4
John 4:10
Eph 2:8

6:5
Ps 34:8
1 Pet 2:3

6:6
2 Pet 2:21
1 Jn 5:16

⁴For it is impossible to bring back to repentance those who were once enlightened— *heaRd* those who have experienced the good things of heaven and shared in the Holy Spirit, ⁵ who have tasted the goodness of the word of God and the power of the age to come—⁶ and who then turn away from God. It is impossible to bring back such people back to repentance; by rejecting the Son of God, they themselves are nailing him to the cross once again and holding him up to public shame. *inability of the law - (bend) NOT STANDING The TEST*

ABRAHAM IN THE NEW TESTAMENT			
Abraham was an ancestor of Jesus Christ.	Matthew 1:1, 2, 17; Luke 3:23, 34	Jesus Christ was human; he was born into the line of Abraham, whom God had chosen to be the father of a great nation through which the whole world would be blessed. We are blessed because of what Jesus Christ, Abraham's descendant, did for us.
Abraham was the father of the Jewish nation.	Matthew 3:9; Luke 3:8; Acts 13:26; Romans 4:1; 11:1; 2 Corinthians 11:22; Hebrews 6:13, 14	God wanted to set apart a nation for himself, a nation that would tell the world about him. He began with a man of faith who, old and childless, believed God's promise of innumerable descendants. We can trust God to do the impossible when we have faith.
Abraham, because of his faith, now sits in the Kingdom with Christ.	Matthew 8:11; Luke 13:28; 16:23-31	Abraham followed God, and now he is enjoying his reward—eternity with God. We will one day meet Abraham because we have been promised eternity as well.
God *is* Abraham's God; thus, Abraham is alive with God.	Matthew 22:32; Mark 12:26; Luke 20:37; Acts 7:32	As Abraham lives forever, we will live forever, because we, like Abraham, have chosen the life of faith.
Abraham received great promises from God.	Luke 1:55, 72, 73; Acts 3:25; 7:17, 18; Galatians 3:6, 14-16; Hebrews 6:13-15	Many of the promises God made to Abraham seemed impossible to be realized, but Abraham trusted God. The promises to believers in God's Word also seem too incredible to believe, but we can trust God to keep all his promises.
Abraham followed God.	Acts 7:2-8; Hebrews 11:8, 17-19	Abraham followed God's leading from his homeland to an unknown territory, which became the Jews' Promised Land. When we follow God, even before he makes all his plans clear to us, we will never be disappointed.
God blessed Abraham because of his faith.	Romans 4; Galatians 3:6-9, 14-19; Hebrews 11:8, 17-19; James 2:21-24	Abraham showed faith in times of disappointment, trial, and testing. Because of Abraham's faith, God counted him righteous and called him his "friend." God accepts us because of our faith.
Abraham is the father of all those who come to God by faith.	Romans 9:6-8; Galatians 3:6-9, 14-29	The Jews are Abraham's children, and Christ was his descendant. We are Christ's brothers and sisters; thus, all believers are Abraham's children and God's children. Abraham was righteous because of his faith; we are made righteous through faith in Christ. The promises made to Abraham apply to us because of Christ.

Priest and the fulfillment of all the Old Testament prophecies. Rather than arguing about the respective merits of Judaism and Christianity, they needed to depend on Christ and live effectively for him.

6:4-6 In the first century, a pagan who investigated Christianity and then went back to paganism made a clean break with the church. But for Jewish Christians who decided to return to Judaism, the break was less obvious. Their lifestyle remained relatively unchanged. But by deliberately turning away from Christ, they were cutting themselves off from God's forgiveness. Those who persevere in believing are true saints; those who continue to reject Christ are unbelievers, no matter how well they behave.

6:6 This verse points to the danger of the Hebrew Christians' returning to Judaism and thus committing apostasy. Some apply this verse today to superficial believers who renounce their Christianity or to unbelievers who come close to salvation and then turn away. Either way, those who reject Christ will not be saved. Christ died once for all. He will not be crucified again. Apart from his cross, there is no other possible way of salvation. However, the author does not indicate that his readers were in danger of renouncing Christ (see 6:9). He is warning against hardness of heart that would make repentance inconceivable for the sinner.

7When the ground soaks up the falling rain and bears a good crop for the farmer, it has God's blessing. 8But if a field bears thorns and thistles, it is useless. The farmer will soon condemn that field and burn it.

9Dear friends, even though we are talking this way, we really don't believe it applies to you. We are confident that you are meant for better things, things that come with salvation. 10For God is not unjust. He will not forget how hard you have worked for him and how you have shown your love to him by caring for other believers,* as you still do. 11Our great desire is that you will keep on loving others as long as life lasts, in order to make certain that what you hope for will come true. 12Then you will not become spiritually dull and indifferent. Instead, you will follow the example of those who are going to inherit God's promises because of their faith and endurance.

God's Promises Bring Hope

13For example, there was God's promise to Abraham. Since there was no one greater to swear by, God took an oath in his own name, saying:

14 "I will certainly bless you,
    and I will multiply your descendants beyond number."*

15Then Abraham waited patiently, and he received what God had promised.

16Now when people take an oath, they call on someone greater than themselves to hold them to it. And without any question that oath is binding. 17God also bound himself with an oath, so that those who received the promise could be perfectly sure that he would never change his mind. 18So God has given both his promise and his oath. These two things are unchangeable because it is impossible for God to lie. Therefore, we who have fled to him for refuge can have great confidence as we hold to the hope that lies before us. 19This hope is a strong and trustworthy anchor for our souls. It leads us through the curtain into God's inner sanctuary. 20Jesus has already gone in there for us. He has become our eternal High Priest in the order of Melchizedek.

Melchizedek Is Greater Than Abraham

7 This Melchizedek was king of the city of Salem and also a priest of God Most High. When Abraham was returning home after winning a great battle against the kings, Melchizedek met him and blessed him. 2Then Abraham took a tenth of all he had captured in battle

6:10 Greek *for God's holy people.*   **6:14** Gen 22:17.

6:8
Gen 3:17-18

6:10
Matt 10:40, 42
1 Thes 1:3

6:11
Heb 3:6; 10:22

6:12
Heb 10:36; 13:7

6:13
Gen 22:16

6:14
†Gen 22:17

6:15
Gen 21:15

6:17
Ps 110:4
Heb 11:9

6:18
Num 23:19
1 Sam 15:29
Titus 1:2
Heb 3:6

6:19
Lev 16:2-3, 12, 15
Heb 9:2-3, 7

6:20
Ps 110:4
Heb 4:14; 5:6

7:1-2
Gen 14:17-20

• **6:7, 8** The writer uses an analogy from agriculture to make a simple point. Real seeds (the gospel) given genuine care by the farmer (God) and planted in a fertile field (your heart and life) will produce a bountiful crop (spiritual maturity). Weeds (temptations) threaten to overwhelm the crop. If the field produces only weeds, then the seeds are lost and the field ruined.

An unproductive Christian life falls under God's condemnation. You have been watered by God's grace with clear and abundant teaching and preaching. What excuse do you have for a useless or unproductive life? Don't be a Christian in name only. Make sure your life bears fruit.

• **6:10** It's easy to get discouraged, thinking that God has forgotten us. But God is never unjust. He never forgets or overlooks our hard work for him. Presently you may not be receiving rewards and acclaim, but God knows your efforts of love and ministry. Let God's love for you and his intimate knowledge of your service for him bolster you as you face disappointment and rejection here on earth.

• **6:11, 12** Hope keeps the Christian from becoming lazy or feeling bored. Like an athlete, train hard and run well, remembering the reward that lies ahead (Philippians 3:14).

6:15 Abraham waited patiently; it was 25 years from the time God had promised him a son (Genesis 12:7; 13:14-16; 15:4, 5; 17:16) to Isaac's birth (Genesis 21:1-3). Because our trials and temptations are often so intense, they seem to last for an eternity. Both the Bible and the testimony of mature Christians encourage us to wait for God to act in his timing, even when our needs seem too great to wait any longer.

6:17 God's promises are unchanging and trustworthy because God is unchanging and trustworthy. When promising Abraham a son, God took an oath in his own name. The oath was as good as God's name, and God's name was as good as his divine nature.

• **6:18, 19** These two unchangeable things are God's promise and his oath. God embodies all truth; therefore, he cannot lie. Because God is truth, you can be secure in his promises; you don't need to wonder if he will change his plans. Our hope is secure and immovable, anchored in God, just as a ship's anchor holds firmly to the seabed. To the true seeker who comes to God in belief, God gives an unconditional promise of acceptance. When you ask God with openness, honesty, and sincerity to save you from your sins, *he will do it*. This truth should give you encouragement, assurance, and confidence.

• **6:19, 20** A curtain hung between the Holy Place and the Most Holy Place, "God's inner sanctuary." This curtain prevented anyone from entering, gazing into, or even getting a fleeting glimpse of the interior of the Most Holy Place (see also 9:1-8). The high priest could enter there only once a year to stand in God's presence and atone for the sins of the entire nation. But Christ is in God's presence at all times, not just once a year, as the High Priest who can continually intercede for us.

7:2ff The writer uses this story from Genesis 14:18-20 to show that Christ is even greater than Abraham, father of the Jewish nation, and Levi (Abraham's descendant). Therefore, the Jewish priesthood (made up of Levi's descendants) was inferior to Melchizedek's priesthood (a type of Christ's priesthood).

7:3
Ps 110:4

and gave it to Melchizedek. The name Melchizedek means "king of justice," and king of Salem means "king of peace." ³There is no record of his father or mother or any of his ancestors—no beginning or end to his life. He remains a priest forever, resembling the Son of God.

7:4
Gen 14:20

7:5
Num 18:21, 26

7:6
Rom 4:13

7:7
Gen 14:19

⁴Consider then how great this Melchizedek was. Even Abraham, the great patriarch of Israel, recognized this by giving him a tenth of what he had taken in battle. ⁵Now the law of Moses required that the priests, who are descendants of Levi, must collect a tithe from the rest of the people of Israel,* who are also descendants of Abraham. ⁶But Melchizedek, who was not a descendant of Levi, collected a tenth from Abraham. And Melchizedek placed a blessing upon Abraham, the one who had already received the promises of God. ⁷And without question, the person who has the power to give a blessing is greater than the one who is blessed.

7:8
Heb 5:6; 6:20

⁸The priests who collect tithes are men who die, so Melchizedek is greater than they are, because we are told that he lives on. ⁹In addition, we might even say that these Levites—the ones who collect the tithe—paid a tithe to Melchizedek when their ancestor Abraham paid a tithe to him. ¹⁰For although Levi wasn't born yet, the seed from which he came was in Abraham's body when Melchizedek collected the tithe from him.

7:11
Ps 110:4
Heb 5:6; 7:17

7:14
Gen 49:10
Isa 11:1
Matt 1:3; 2:6
Luke 3:33
Rom 1:3
Rev 5:5

¹¹So if the priesthood of Levi, on which the law was based, could have achieved the perfection God intended, why did God need to establish a different priesthood, with a priest in the order of Melchizedek instead of the order of Levi and Aaron?*

¹²And if the priesthood is changed, the law must also be changed to permit it. ¹³For the priest we are talking about belongs to a different tribe, whose members have never served at the altar as priests. ¹⁴What I mean is, our Lord came from the tribe of Judah, and Moses never mentioned priests coming from that tribe.

Jesus Is like Melchizedek

¹⁵This change has been made very clear since a different priest, who is like Melchizedek, has appeared. ¹⁶Jesus became a priest, not by meeting the physical requirement of be-

7:17
†Ps 110:4
Heb 5:6; 6:20

longing to the tribe of Levi, but by the power of a life that cannot be destroyed. ¹⁷And the psalmist pointed this out when he prophesied,

"You are a priest forever in the order of Melchizedek."*

7:18
Rom 8:3

7:19
Rom 3:20
Heb 9:9; 10:19-22

¹⁸Yes, the old requirement about the priesthood was set aside because it was weak and useless. ¹⁹For the law never made anything perfect. But now we have confidence in a better hope, through which we draw near to God.

7:21
†Ps 110:4
Heb 5:6; 6:20; 7:17

²⁰This new system was established with a solemn oath. Aaron's descendants became priests without such an oath, ²¹but there was an oath regarding Jesus. For God said to him,

"The LORD has taken an oath and will not break his vow:
'You are a priest forever.'"*

7:5 Greek *from their brothers.*   **7:11** Greek *the order of Aaron?*   **7:17** Ps 110:4.   **7:21** Ps 110:4.

• **7:3-10** Melchizedek was a priest of God Most High (see the note on Genesis 14:18 and his Profile in Genesis 15, p. 29). He is said to remain a priest forever (see also Psalm 110:4), because his priesthood has no record of beginning or ending. He was a priest of God in Salem (Jerusalem) long before the nation of Israel and the regular priesthood began.

• **7:11-17** Jesus' high-priestly role was superior to that of any priest of Levi, because the Messiah was a priest of a higher order (Psalm 110:4). If the Jewish priests and their laws had been able to save people, why would God need to send Christ as a priest, who came not from the tribe of Levi (the priestly tribe) but from the tribe of Judah? The animal sacrifices had to be repeated, and they offered only temporary forgiveness; but Christ's sacrifice was offered once, and it offers total and permanent forgiveness. Under the new covenant, the Levitical priesthood was canceled in favor of Christ's role as High Priest. Because Christ is our High Priest, we need to pay attention to him. No minister, leader, or Christian friend can substitute for Christ's work and for his role in our salvation.

7:18, 19 The law was not intended to save people or to make them perfect, but to point out sin (see Romans 3:20; 5:20) and to point toward Christ (see Galatians 3:24, 25). Salvation comes through Christ, whose sacrifice brings forgiveness for our sins. Being ethical, working diligently to help others, and giving to charitable causes are all commendable, but all of our good deeds cannot save us or make us right with God.

7:19 How can you draw near to God? The Bible makes it clear that your own body is God's temple. Your spirit needs and wants closeness with God. You want to know the living God personally, not as an idea or concept, not as a distant monarch. You can draw near to God through prayer, worship, and Bible meditation. You need not live like a monk, but you probably need more prayer in your life. The habit of worship has become a convenience to be wedged between sports and other recreations. Instead, make worship your top priority. Bible meditation may include verse memory, songs, and quiet personal reading. The Bible is the word of God for you. Use it every day and you will draw nearer and nearer to God.

22Because of this oath, Jesus is the one who guarantees this better covenant with God.

23There were many priests under the old system, for death prevented them from remaining in office. 24But because Jesus lives forever, his priesthood lasts forever. 25Therefore he is able, once and forever, to save* those who come to God through him. He lives forever to intercede with God on their behalf.

26He is the kind of high priest we need because he is holy and blameless, unstained by sin. He has been set apart from sinners and has been given the highest place of honor in heaven.* 27Unlike those other high priests, he does not need to offer sacrifices every day. They did this for their own sins first and then for the sins of the people. But Jesus did this once for all when he offered himself as the sacrifice for the people's sins. 28The law appointed high priests who were limited by human weakness. But after the law was given, God appointed his Son with an oath, and his Son has been made the perfect High Priest forever.

4. The new covenant is greater than the old
Christ Is Our High Priest

8 Here is the main point: We have a High Priest who sat down in the place of honor beside the throne of the majestic God in heaven. 2There he ministers in the heavenly Tabernacle,* the true place of worship that was built by the Lord and not by human hands.

3And since every high priest is required to offer gifts and sacrifices, our High Priest must make an offering, too. 4If he were here on earth, he would not even be a priest, since there already are priests who offer the gifts required by the law. 5They serve in a system of worship that is only a copy, a shadow of the real one in heaven. For when Moses was getting ready to build the Tabernacle, God gave him this warning: "Be sure that you make everything according to the pattern I have shown you here on the mountain."*

6But now Jesus, our High Priest, has been given a ministry that is far superior to the old priesthood, for he is the one who mediates for us a far better covenant with God, based on better promises.

7:22 Heb 8:6; 12:24
7:24 Isa 9:6-7; Rev 1:18
7:25 Rom 8:34; 1 Jn 2:1
7:26 2 Cor 5:21; Heb 4:14
7:27 Lev 9:7; 16:6, 11, 15; Eph 5:2; Heb 9:12
7:28 Heb 2:10; 5:1-2
8:1 Heb 1:3; 2:17; 4:14; 6:20; 7:26; 9:11
8:2 Heb 9:11
8:3 Heb 5:1
8:5 †Exod 25:40; 26:30; Col 2:17; Heb 9:23
8:6 Heb 7:22; 9:15; 12:24

7:25 Or *is able to save completely.*   **7:26** Or *has been exalted higher than the heavens.*   **8:2** Or *tent;* also in 8:5.
8:5 Exod 25:40; 26:30.

• **7:22-24** Jesus has a permanent priesthood. He should be everyone's ultimate authority for spiritual life. In our culture today, however, many people have advisers and counselors whom they elevate almost to the role of priest. People look to political leaders, lawyers, physicians, insurance agents, and financial advisers to provide hope, long life, and security against all disasters. Many Christians regard the advice of priests and ministers, Christian friends, and even pop musicians before they consider the words of Jesus written in the Bible. Make sure your first allegiance and priority is to know and follow the advice given by Jesus.

• **7:25** No one can add to what Jesus did to save us; our past, present, and future sins are all forgiven, and Jesus is with the Father as a sign that our sins are forgiven. As our High Priest, Christ is our Advocate, the mediator between us and God. He looks after our interests and intercedes for us with God. The Old Testament high priest went before God once a year to plead for the forgiveness of the nation's sins; Christ makes perpetual intercession before God for us. Christ's continuous presence in heaven with the Father assures us that our sins have been paid for and forgiven (see Romans 8:33, 34; Hebrews 2:17, 18; 4:15, 16; 9:24). This wonderful assurance frees us from guilt and from fear of failure. If you are a Christian, remember that Christ has paid the price for your sins once and for all (see also 9:24-28).

• **7:27** In Old Testament times when animals were sacrificed, they were cut into pieces, the parts were washed, the fat was burned, the blood was sprinkled, and the meat was boiled. Blood was demanded as atonement for sin, and God accepted animal blood to cover the people's sin (Leviticus 17:11). Because of the sacrificial system, the Israelites were generally aware that sin costs someone something and that they themselves were sinful. Many people take Christ's work on the cross for granted. They don't realize how costly it was for Jesus to secure our forgiveness—

it cost him his life and painful, temporary separation from his Father (Matthew 27:46; 1 Peter 1:18, 19).

Because Jesus died *once for all,* he brought the sacrificial system to an end. He forgave sins—past, present, and future. The Jews did not need to go back to the old system because Christ, the perfect sacrifice, completed the work of redemption. You don't have to look for another way to have your sins forgiven—Christ was the final sacrifice for you.

• **7:28** So much is attributed to Jesus in this chapter that it might appear that there is nothing you need to do, or can do, to make salvation a reality for you. And that is true. Jesus has done it all. Nothing you do can improve his work. Nothing you do adds to God's acceptance of Jesus' sacrifice.

So how do the benefits of Jesus' sacrifice become yours? You accept the gift of salvation by faith, trusting entirely in Jesus for salvation. You can do that now through a simple prayer: "Dear God, I trust in Jesus alone. Please forgive my sins through him, and give me the eternal life secured by him. Amen."

• **8:4** Under the old Jewish system, priests were chosen only from the tribe of Levi, and sacrifices were offered daily on the altar for forgiveness of sins (see 7:12-14). This system would not have allowed Jesus to be a priest, because he was from the tribe of Judah. But his perfect sacrifice ended all need for further priests and sacrifices.

The use of the present tense, "there already are priests who offer the gifts," indicates that this book was written before A.D. 70 when the Temple in Jerusalem was destroyed, ending the sacrifices.

8:5 The pattern for the Tabernacle built by Moses was given by God. It was a pattern of the spiritual reality of Christ's sacrifice, and thus it looked forward to the future reality. There is no Tabernacle in heaven of which the earthly one is a copy, but rather the earthly Tabernacle was an expression of eternal, theological principles. Because the Temple at Jerusalem had not yet been destroyed, using the worship system there as an example would have had a great impact on this original audience.

8:7
Heb 7:11
8:8-12
†Jer 31:31-34

⁷If the first covenant had been faultless, there would have been no need for a second covenant to replace it. ⁸But when God found fault with the people, he said:

> "The day is coming, says the LORD,
>   when I will make a new covenant
>   with the people of Israel and Judah.
> ⁹ This covenant will not be like the one
>   I made with their ancestors
> when I took them by the hand
>   and led them out of the land of Egypt.
> They did not remain faithful to my covenant,
>   so I turned my back on them, says the LORD.

8:10
Heb 10:16

> ¹⁰ But this is the new covenant I will make
>   with the people of Israel on that day,* says the LORD:
> I will put my laws in their minds,
>   and I will write them on their hearts.
> I will be their God,
>   and they will be my people.

8:11
John 6:45

> ¹¹ And they will not need to teach their neighbors,
>   nor will they need to teach their relatives,*
> saying, 'You should know the LORD.'

8:10 Greek *after those days.*   **8:11** Greek *their brother.*

THE OLD AND NEW COVENANTS

Like pointing out the similarities and differences between the photograph of a person and the actual person, the writer of Hebrews shows the connection between the old Mosaic covenant and the new Messianic covenant. He proves that the old covenant was a shadow of the real Christ.

Reference	The Old Covenant under Moses	The New Covenant in Christ	Application
8:3-4	Gifts and sacrifices by those guilty of sin	Self-sacrifice by the guiltless Christ	Christ died for you
8:5-6, 10-12	Focused on a physical building where one goes to worship	Focuses on the reign of Christ in believers' hearts	God is directly involved in your life
8:5-6, 10-12	A shadow	A reality	Not temporal, but eternal
8:6	Limited promises	Limitless promises	We can trust God's promises to us
8:8-9	Failed agreement by people	Faithful agreement by Christ	Christ has kept the agreement where people couldn't
9:1	External standards and rules	Internal standards— a new heart	God sees both actions and motives—we are accountable to God, not rules
9:7	Limited access to God	Unlimited access to God	God is personally available
9:9-10	Legal cleansing	Personal cleansing	God's cleansing is complete
9:11-14; 24-28	Continual sacrifice	Conclusive sacrifice	Christ's sacrifice was perfect and final
9:22	Forgiveness earned	Forgiveness freely given	We have true and complete forgiveness
9:24-28	Repeated yearly	Completed by Christ's death	Christ's death can be applied to our sin
9:26	Available to some	Available to all	Available to you

• **8:8-12** This passage is a quotation of Jeremiah 31:31-34, which compares the new covenant with the old. The old covenant was the covenant of law between God and Israel. The new and better way is the covenant of grace—Christ's offer to forgive our sins and bring us to God through his sacrificial death. This covenant is new in extent—it goes beyond Israel and Judah to include all the Gentile nations. It is new in application because it is written on our heart and in our mind. It offers a new way to forgiveness, not through animal sacrifice but through faith. Have you entered into this new covenant and begun walking in the better way?

• **8:10** If our heart is not changed, following God's rules will be unpleasant and difficult. We will rebel against being told how to live. The Holy Spirit, however, gives us new desires, helping us *want* to obey God (see Philippians 2:12, 13). With a new heart, we find that serving God is our greatest joy.

• **8:10, 11** Under God's new covenant, God's law is inside us. It is no longer an external set of rules and principles. The Holy Spirit reminds us of Christ's words, activates our conscience, influences our motives and desires, and makes us want to obey. Now doing God's will is something we desire with all our heart and mind.

For everyone, from the least to the greatest,
　　will know me already.
12 And I will forgive their wickedness,
　　and I will never again remember their sins."*

8:12
Heb 10:17

13 When God speaks of a "new" covenant, it means he has made the first one obsolete. It is now out of date and will soon disappear.

8:13
Heb 12:24

Old Rules about Worship

9 That first covenant between God and Israel had regulations for worship and a place of worship here on earth. 2 There were two rooms in that Tabernacle.* In the first room were a lampstand, a table, and sacred loaves of bread on the table. This room was called the Holy Place. 3 Then there was a curtain, and behind the curtain was the second room* called the Most Holy Place. 4 In that room were a gold incense altar and a wooden chest called the Ark of the Covenant, which was covered with gold on all sides. Inside the Ark were a gold jar containing manna, Aaron's staff that sprouted leaves, and the stone tablets of the covenant. 5 Above the Ark were the cherubim of divine glory, whose wings stretched out over the Ark's cover, the place of atonement. But we cannot explain these things in detail now.

9:2
Exod 25:23-40;
26:1-30
Lev 24:5
9:3
Exod 26:31-33
9:4
Exod 16:33;
25:10-16; 30:1-6
Num 17:8-10
Deut 10:3-5
9:5
Exod 25:17-22

6 When these things were all in place, the priests regularly entered the first room* as they performed their religious duties. 7 But only the high priest ever entered the Most Holy Place, and only once a year. And he always offered blood for his own sins and for the sins the people had committed in ignorance. 8 By these regulations the Holy Spirit revealed that the entrance to the Most Holy Place was not freely open as long as the Tabernacle* and the system it represented were still in use.

9:6
Num 18:2-6
9:7
Exod 30:10
Lev 16:2, 14-15
Heb 5:2-3
9:8
John 14:6
Heb 10:19-20

9 This is an illustration pointing to the present time. For the gifts and sacrifices that the priests offer are not able to cleanse the consciences of the people who bring them. 10 For that old system deals only with food and drink and various cleansing ceremonies—physical regulations that were in effect only until a better system could be established.

9:9
Heb 5:1; 10:1-2
9:10
Lev 11:2, 25; 15:8
Num 6:3; 19:13

Christ Is the Perfect Sacrifice

11 So Christ has now become the High Priest over all the good things that have come.* He has entered that greater, more perfect Tabernacle in heaven, which was not made by human hands and is not part of this created world. 12 With his own blood—not the blood of goats and calves—he entered the Most Holy Place once for all time and secured our redemption forever.

9:11
Heb 8:2; 10:1
9:12
Heb 7:27

8:8-12 Jer 31:31-34.　**9:2** Or *tent;* also in 9:11, 21.　**9:3** Greek *second tent.*　**9:6** Greek *first tent.*　**9:8** Or *the first room;* Greek reads *the first tent.*　**9:11** Some manuscripts read *that are about to come.*

8:13 Some of the Jewish believers were clinging to the obsolete old ways instead of embracing Christ's new covenant. All the joy of newfound faith and all the relief of fresh forgiveness had given way to a kind of boredom that was never supposed to be. Growth had stopped. What should be done if this happens to you?

Realize that life in Christ is never complete. Heaven promises completeness; until then, growth is the normal pattern. Growth often endures seasons of drought and drabness. That's also normal. Think about what you are doing that might be spiritually ineffective or obsolete. The key to growth includes daily devotion to Christ through Bible study and prayer. Perhaps you need to intensify your study and find helps that provide more substance. Perhaps you need to grow by engaging in new areas of service that express your faith. Seek God for how he would have you keep growing in your faith.

9:5 "Cherubim" are mighty angels. One of the functions of the cherubim was to serve as guardians. These angels guarded the entrances to both the tree of life (Genesis 3:24) and the Most Holy Place (Exodus 26:31-33). With their wings "stretched out over the Ark's cover, the place of atonement," these two gold statues were believed to support God's invisible presence (Ezekiel 9:3; 10:4, 18). Here they are called "the cherubim of divine glory," referring to God's glory which hovered over the Ark of the Covenant (Exodus 40:34-36; Leviticus 16:2).

• **9:6-8** The high priest could enter the Most Holy Place (9:3), the innermost room of the Tabernacle, one day each year to atone for the nation's sins. The Most Holy Place was a small room that contained the Ark of the Covenant (a gold-covered chest containing the original stone tablets on which the Ten Commandments were written, a jar of manna, and Aaron's staff). The top of the chest served as the "atonement cover" (the altar) on which the blood would be sprinkled by the high priest on the Day of Atonement. The Most Holy Place was the most sacred spot on earth for the Jews and only the high priest could enter it. The other priests and the common people were forbidden to come into the room. Their only access to God was through the high priest, who would offer a sacrifice and use the animal's blood to atone first for his own sins and then for the people's sins (see also 10:19).

9:10 The people had to keep the Old Testament dietary laws and ceremonial cleansing laws until Christ came with God's new and better way.

9:12 This imagery comes from the Day of Atonement rituals described in Leviticus 16. Through his own death, Christ freed us from the slavery of sin forever.

• **9:12-14** Though you know Christ, you may believe that you have to work hard to make yourself good enough for God. But rules and rituals have never cleansed people's hearts. By Jesus' blood alone (1) we have our conscience cleansed, (2) we are freed from death's sting and can live to serve God, and (3) we are freed from sin's power. If you are carrying a load of guilt because you are finding that you can't be good enough for God, take another look at Jesus' death and what it means for you. Christ can heal your

9:13
Lev 16:3, 14-15
Num 19:9, 17

9:14
Heb 6:1
1 Pet 3:18
1 Jn 1:7

9:15
1 Tim 2:5
Heb 7:22

13Under the old system, the blood of goats and bulls and the ashes of a young cow could cleanse people's bodies from ceremonial impurity. 14Just think how much more the blood of Christ will purify our consciences from sinful deeds* so that we can worship the living God. For by the power of the eternal Spirit, Christ offered himself to God as a perfect sacrifice for our sins. 15That is why he is the one who mediates a new covenant between God and people, so that all who are called can receive the eternal inheritance God has promised them. For Christ died to set them free from the penalty of the sins they had committed under that first covenant.

16Now when someone leaves a will,* it is necessary to prove that the person who made it is dead.* 17The will goes into effect only after the person's death. While the person who made it is still alive, the will cannot be put into effect.

9:18-19
Exod 24:6-8
Lev 14:4
Num 19:6

9:20
†Exod 24:8
Matt 26:28

9:21
Lev 8:15, 19

9:22
Lev 17:11

9:23
Heb 8:5

18That is why even the first covenant was put into effect with the blood of an animal. 19For after Moses had read each of God's commandments to all the people, he took the blood of calves and goats,* along with water, and sprinkled both the book of God's law and all the people, using hyssop branches and scarlet wool. 20Then he said, "This blood confirms the covenant God has made with you."* 21And in the same way, he sprinkled blood on the Tabernacle and on everything used for worship. 22In fact, according to the law of Moses, nearly everything was purified with blood. For without the shedding of blood, there is no forgiveness.

23That is why the Tabernacle and everything in it, which were copies of things in heaven, had to be purified by the blood of animals. But the real things in heaven had to be purified with far better sacrifices than the blood of animals.

9:24
Rom 8:34
Heb 8:2; 9:12
1 Jn 2:1

9:25
Heb 9:7; 10:19

9:26
1 Cor 10:11
Heb 7:27
1 Pet 3:18

24For Christ did not enter into a holy place made with human hands, which was only a copy of the true one in heaven. He entered into heaven itself to appear now before God on our behalf. 25And he did not enter heaven to offer himself again and again, like the high priest here on earth who enters the Most Holy Place year after year with the blood of an animal. 26If that had been necessary, Christ would have had to die again and again, ever since the world began. But now, once for all time, he has appeared at the end of the age* to remove sin by his own death as a sacrifice.

9:14 Greek *from dead works.*   **9:16a** Or *covenant;* also in 9:17.   **9:16b** Or *Now when someone makes a covenant, it is necessary to ratify it with the death of a sacrifice.*   **9:19** Some manuscripts do not include *and goats.*
9:20 Exod 24:8.   **9:26** Greek *the ages.*

conscience and deliver you from the frustration of trying to earn God's favor. Bring your guilt-ridden life to Christ, confess your inability to clean up your own conscience, ask him to forgive you. Thank him for his deliverance. God can forgive you and clear your record.

• **9:13, 14** When the people sacrificed animals, God considered the people's faith and obedience, cleansed them from sin, and made them *ceremonially* acceptable according to Old Testament law. But Christ's sacrifice transforms our lives and hearts and makes us clean on the inside. His sacrifice is infinitely more effective than animal sacrifices. No barrier of sin or weakness on our part can stifle his forgiveness.

9:14 Sinful deeds are more than just wrong actions; ironically, these also include our attempts to reach God by being good enough! Our culture glorifies self-effort and personal achievement. It defines a successful person as one who obtains certain goals: financial security, health and fitness, and the respect of others. But here the Bible gives us a different picture of successful living: accept Jesus' sacrifice for your sin, abandon the futility of sinful deeds, and let the blood of Christ purify your conscience (see 10:19-22).

• **9:15** People in Old Testament times were saved through Christ's sacrifice, although that sacrifice had not yet happened. In offering unblemished animal sacrifices, they were anticipating Christ's coming and his death for sin. There was no point in returning to the sacrificial system now that Christ had come and had become the final, perfect sacrifice.

• **9:22** Why does forgiveness require the shedding of blood? This is no arbitrary decree on the part of a bloodthirsty God, as some have suggested. There is no greater symbol of life than blood; blood keeps us alive. Jesus shed his blood—gave his life—for our

sins so that we wouldn't have to experience spiritual death, eternal separation from God. Jesus is the source of life, not death. He gave his own life to pay our penalty for us so that we might live. After shedding his blood for us, Christ rose from the grave and proclaimed victory over sin and death.

9:23 In a way that we don't fully understand, the earthly Tabernacle was a copy and symbol of heavenly realities. This purification of the heavenly things can best be understood as referring to Christ's spiritual work for us in heaven (see the note on 8:5).

9:24 Among references to priests, Tabernacles, sacrifices, and other ideas unfamiliar to us, we come to this description of Christ appearing in God's presence on our behalf. We can relate to this role and be encouraged by it. Christ is on our side at God's side. He is our Lord and Savior. He is not there to convince or remind God that our sins are forgiven but to present both our needs and our service for him as an offering (see 7:25).

• **9:24-28** All people die physically, but Christ died so that we would not have to die spiritually. We can have wonderful confidence in his saving work for us, doing away with sin—past, present, and future. He has forgiven our past sin—when he died on the cross, he sacrificed himself once for all (9:26); he has given us the Holy Spirit to help us deal with present sin; he appears before God for us now in heaven (9:24); and he promises to return (9:28) and raise us to eternal life in a world where sin will be banished.

9:26 The "end of the age" refers to the time of Christ's coming to earth in fulfillment of the Old Testament prophecies. Christ ushered in the new era of grace and forgiveness. We are still living in the "end of the age." The day of the Lord has begun and will be completed at Christ's return.

27 And just as each person is destined to die once and after that comes judgment, 28 so also Christ died once for all time as a sacrifice to take away the sins of many people. He will come again, not to deal with our sins, but to bring salvation to all who are eagerly waiting for him.

Christ's Sacrifice Once for All

10 The old system under the law of Moses was only a shadow, a dim preview of the good things to come, not the good things themselves. The sacrifices under that system were repeated again and again, year after year, but they were never able to provide perfect cleansing for those who came to worship. 2If they could have provided perfect cleansing, the sacrifices would have stopped, for the worshipers would have been purified once for all time, and their feelings of guilt would have disappeared.

3But instead, those sacrifices actually reminded them of their sins year after year. 4For it is not possible for the blood of bulls and goats to take away sins. 5That is why, when Christ* came into the world, he said to God,

"You did not want animal sacrifices or sin offerings.
　　But you have given me a body to offer.
6 You were not pleased with burnt offerings
　　or other offerings for sin.
7 Then I said, 'Look, I have come to do your will, O God—
　　as is written about me in the Scriptures.'"*

8First, Christ said, "You did not want animal sacrifices or sin offerings or burnt offerings or other offerings for sin, nor were you pleased with them" (though they are required by the law of Moses). 9Then he said, "Look, I have come to do your will." He cancels the first covenant in order to put the second into effect. 10For God's will was for us to be made holy by the sacrifice of the body of Jesus Christ, once for all time.

11Under the old covenant, the priest stands and ministers before the altar day after day, offering the same sacrifices again and again, which can never take away sins. 12But our High

10:5 Greek *he;* also in 10:8.　**10:5-7** Ps 40:6-8 (Greek version).

9:27
Gen 3:19
9:28
Isa 53:12
Phil 3:20
Heb 7:27
1 Pet 2:24
10:1
Col 2:17
Heb 7:19; 8:5; 9:11
10:3
Lev 16:34
Heb 9:7
10:4
Lev 16:15, 21
Heb 9:13
10:5-7
†Ps 40:6-8
10:8
†Ps 40:6
10:10
Eph 5:2
Heb 7:27; 9:12, 28
1 Pet 2:24
10:11
Heb 5:1
10:12
Ps 110:1
Matt 22:44
Col 3:1
Heb 1:3

9:27 Judgment is not a popular theme today, but the Bible teaches that judgment is coming. Do you look forward to Christ's return, or do you see it as a threat? As sure as death itself, judgment awaits. At God's judgment there will be no higher court of appeal should the verdict not be to your liking. If you hope for a favorable verdict in this court, put your hope entirely on Jesus. Pray today—now if you haven't before—for the freedom and pardon Jesus has won for you. Then rejoice that God's judgment of you will be based on the perfect life of his Son, Jesus. After that, tell others, for many will face an unfavorable judgment without Jesus.

• **10:3** When people gathered for the offering of sacrifices on the Day of Atonement, they were reminded of their sins, and they undoubtedly felt guilty all over again. What they needed most was forgiveness—the permanent, powerful, sin-destroying forgiveness we have from Christ. When we confess a sin to him, we need never think of it again. Christ has forgiven us, and the sin no longer exists. See 1 John 1:9.

• **10:4** Animal sacrifices could not take away sins; they provided only a temporary way to deal with sin until Jesus came to deal with sin permanently. How, then, were people forgiven in Old Testament times? Because Old Testament believers were following God's command to offer sacrifices, he graciously forgave them when, by faith, they made their sacrifices. But that practice looked forward to Christ's perfect sacrifice. Christ's way was superior to the Old Testament way because the old way only pointed to what Christ would do to take away sins.

10:5-10 This quotation is not cited in any other New Testament book. However, it is a central teaching of the Old Testament that God desires obedience and a right heart, not empty compliance with the sacrifice system (see the chart in Hosea 7, p. 1413). The writer of Hebrews applies to Christ the words of the psalmist in Psalm 40:6-8. Christ came to offer his body on the cross for us as a sacrifice that is completely acceptable to God. God's new and living way for us to please him is not by keeping laws or even by abstain-

ing from sin. It is by coming to him in faith to be forgiven, and then following him in loving obedience.

• **10:5-10** The costly sacrifice of an animal's life impressed upon the sinner the seriousness of his or her own sin before God. Because Jesus shed his own blood for us, his sacrifice is infinitely greater than any Old Testament offering. Considering the immeasurable gift he gave us, we should respond by giving him our devotion and service.

10:9 Canceling the first covenant in order to put into effect a far better one meant doing away with the system of sacrifices contained in the ceremonial law. It didn't mean eliminating God's *moral* law (the Ten Commandments). The ceremonial law prepared people for Christ's coming. With Christ's death and resurrection, that system was no longer needed. And through Christ we can fulfill the moral law as we let him live in us.

• **10:11, 12** Christ's work is contrasted with the work of the Jewish priests. The priests' work was never finished, so they had to stand day after day and offer sacrifices; Christ's sacrifice (dying in our place) is finished, so he is seated. The priests repeated the sacrifices often; Christ sacrificed once for all. The sacrifice system couldn't completely remove sin; Christ's sacrifice effectively cleansed us.

• **10:12** If the Jewish readers of this book were to return to the old Jewish system, they would be implying that Christ's sacrifice wasn't enough to forgive their sins. Adding anything to his sacrifice or taking anything from it denies its validity. Any system to gain salvation through good deeds is essentially rejecting the significance of Christ's death and spurning the Holy Spirit's work. Beware of anyone who tells you that Christ's sacrifice still leaves you incomplete or that something else is needed to make you acceptable to God. When we believe in Christ, he makes us completely right with God. Our loving relationship leads us to follow him in willing obedience and service. He is pleased with our service, but we cannot be saved by our good deeds.

Priest offered himself to God as a single sacrifice for sins, good for all time. Then he sat down in the place of honor at God's right hand. [13]There he waits until his enemies are humbled and made a footstool under his feet. [14]For by that one offering he forever made perfect those who are being made holy.

[15]And the Holy Spirit also testifies that this is so. For he says,

[16] "This is the new covenant I will make
    with my people on that day,* says the LORD:
I will put my laws in their hearts,
    and I will write them on their minds."*

[17]Then he says,

    "I will never again remember
        their sins and lawless deeds."*

[18]And when sins have been forgiven, there is no need to offer any more sacrifices.

B. THE SUPERIORITY OF FAITH (10:19—13:25)

Moving from argument to instruction, the author cites many examples of those who have demonstrated faith throughout history. Living by faith is far better than merely fulfilling rituals and rules. This can challenge us to grow in faith and to live in obedience to God each day.

A Call to Persevere

[19]And so, dear brothers and sisters,* we can boldly enter heaven's Most Holy Place because of the blood of Jesus. [20]By his death,* Jesus opened a new and life-giving way through the curtain into the Most Holy Place. [21]And since we have a great High Priest who rules over God's house, [22]let us go right into the presence of God with sincere hearts fully trusting him. For our guilty consciences have been sprinkled with Christ's blood to make us clean, and our bodies have been washed with pure water.

[23]Let us hold tightly without wavering to the hope we affirm, for God can be trusted to keep his promise. [24]Let us think of ways to motivate one another to acts of love and good works. [25]And let us not neglect our meeting together, as some people do, but encourage one another, especially now that the day of his return is drawing near.

10:16a Greek *after those days.* **10:16b** Jer 31:33a. **10:17** Jer 31:34b. **10:19** Greek *brothers.* **10:20** Greek *Through his flesh.*

Cross references (left margin):
10:13 Ps 110:1
10:15 Heb 3:7
10:16-17 †Jer 31:33-34
10:19 Eph 3:12
10:20 John 4:6; Heb 6:19; 9:8
10:21 Heb 2:17; 3:6
10:22 Ezek 36:25; Eph 5:26
10:23 1 Cor 1:9; 10:13; Heb 3:6
10:25 Acts 2:42; Heb 3:13

10:14 We have been made perfect, yet we are being made holy. Through his death and resurrection, Christ, once for all, made his believers perfect in God's sight. At the same time, he is making them holy (progressively cleansed and set apart for his special use) in their daily pilgrimage here. We should not be surprised, ashamed, or shocked that we still need to grow. God is not finished with us. We can encourage this growth process by deliberately applying Scripture to all areas of our life, by accepting the discipline and guidance Christ provides, and by giving him control of our desires and goals.

• **10:17** The writer concludes his argument with this powerful statement that God will never again remember our sins. Christ forgives completely, so there is no need to confess our past sins repeatedly. As believers, we can be confident that the sins we confess and renounce are forgiven and forgotten.

10:19 The Most Holy Place in the Temple was sealed from view by a curtain (10:20). Only the high priest could enter this holy room, and he did so only once a year on the Day of Atonement when he offered the sacrifice for the nation's sins. But Jesus' death removed the curtain, and all believers may walk into God's presence at any time (see also 6:19, 20).

10:21, 22 How is it possible for us to go right into the presence of God? We come not halfheartedly or with improper motives or pretense, but with pure, individual, and sincere worship. We can know that we have "sincere hearts" if we evaluate our thoughts and motives according to his Word (see 4:12). Christians can approach God boldly, free from our "guilty consciences" and in full assurance because of the work of Jesus Christ. We can go to God without doubting, knowing that he will hear and answer

us. Under the new covenant, our hearts and consciences are cleansed completely, not partially or temporarily (see 9:14). Our clean consciences allow us to enter God's presence with boldness. Finally, the imagery of our bodies having been "washed with pure water" actually pictures an inward cleansing. Just as baptism is an outward sign that represents the purification that Christ does inside us, so this washing speaks of an internal cleansing from sin. Once cleansed, we can approach God.

10:22-25 We have significant privileges associated with our new life in Christ: (1) We have personal access to God through Christ and can draw near to him without an elaborate system (10:22); (2) we may grow in faith, overcome doubts and questions, and deepen our relationship with God (10:23); (3) we may enjoy motivation from one another (10:24); (4) we may worship together (10:25).

• **10:25** To neglect Christian meetings is to give up the encouragement and help of other Christians. We gather together to share our faith and to strengthen one another in the Lord. As we get closer to the day when Christ will return, we will face many spiritual struggles, and even times of persecution. Anti-Christian forces will grow in strength. Difficulties should never be excuses for missing church services. Rather, as difficulties arise, we should make an even greater effort to be faithful in attendance.

26 Dear friends, if we deliberately continue sinning after we have received knowledge of the truth, there is no longer any sacrifice that will cover these sins. 27 There is only the terrible expectation of God's judgment and the raging fire that will consume his enemies. 28 For anyone who refused to obey the law of Moses was put to death without mercy on the testimony of two or three witnesses. 29 Just think how much worse the punishment will be for those who have trampled on the Son of God, and have treated the blood of the covenant, which made us holy, as if it were common and unholy, and have insulted and disdained the Holy Spirit who brings God's mercy to us. 30 For we know the one who said,

> "I will take revenge.
> I will pay them back."*

He also said,

> "The Lord will judge his own people."*

31 It is a terrible thing to fall into the hands of the living God.

32 Think back on those early days when you first learned about Christ.* Remember how you remained faithful even though it meant terrible suffering. 33 Sometimes you were exposed to public ridicule and were beaten, and sometimes you helped others who were suffering the same things. 34 You suffered along with those who were thrown into jail, and when all you owned was taken from you, you accepted it with joy. You knew there were better things waiting for you that will last forever.

35 So do not throw away this confident trust in the Lord. Remember the great reward it brings you! 36 Patient endurance is what you need now, so that you will continue to do God's will. Then you will receive all that he has promised.

37 "For in just a little while,
> the Coming One will come and not delay.
38 And my righteous ones will live by faith.*
> But I will take no pleasure in anyone who turns away."*

39 But we are not like those who turn away from God to their own destruction. We are the faithful ones, whose souls will be saved.

10:26 Heb 6:4-8
2 Pet 2:20

10:27 Isa 26:11

10:28 Deut 17:6

10:30 †Deut 32:35-36
Ps 135:14

10:31 2 Cor 5:11

10:33 1 Cor 4:9
1 Thes 2:14

10:34 Heb 13:3

10:36 Heb 9:15

10:37-38 †Hab 2:3-4
Rom 1:17
Gal 3:11

10:30a Deut 32:35.   **10:30b** Deut 32:36.   **10:32** Greek *when you were first enlightened.*   **10:38** Or *my righteous ones will live by their faithfulness;* Greek reads *my righteous one will live by faith.*   **10:37-38** Hab 2:3-4.

10:26 When people deliberately reject Christ's offer of salvation, they reject God's most precious gift. They ignore the leading of the Holy Spirit, the one who communicates to us God's saving love. This warning was given to Jewish Christians who were tempted to reject Christ for Judaism, but it applies to anyone who rejects Christ for another religion or, having understood Christ's atoning work, deliberately turns away from it (see also Numbers 15:30, 31 and Mark 3:28-30). The point is that there is no other acceptable sacrifice for sin than the death of Christ on the cross. If someone deliberately rejects the sacrifice of Christ after clearly understanding the Good News teaching about it, then there is no way for that person to be saved, because God has not provided any other name in all of heaven for people to call on to save them (see Acts 4:12).

10:29 How have people insulted and disdained the Holy Spirit? The sacrifice of Christ is tied with the Holy Spirit; therefore, to scorn Christ's sacrifice is to insult and disdain the Holy Spirit by arrogantly rejecting him. The Holy Spirit is a person, not just a force or influence. To reject him is to cut off the means of God's acceptance. This is equivalent to blasphemy against the Holy Spirit (see Matthew 12:31, 32). Deserving of great punishment are those who insult the Holy Spirit who brings God's mercy.

10:31 God's power is awesome, and his punishment terrible. These words give us a glimpse into the holiness of God. He is sovereign; his power is unlimited; he will do as he promises. This judgment is for those who have rejected God's mercy. For them, falling into God's hands will be a dreadful experience. They will have no more excuses. They will discover that they were wrong, but it will be too late. For those who accept Christ's love and his

salvation, however, the coming judgment is no cause for worry. Being saved through his grace, they have nothing to fear (see 1 John 4:18).

• **10:32-36** Hebrews encourages believers to persevere in their Christian faith and conduct when facing persecution and pressure. We don't usually think of suffering as good for us, but it can build our character and our patience. During times of great stress, we may feel God's presence more clearly and find help from Christians we never thought would care. Knowing that Jesus is with us in our suffering and that he will return one day to put an end to all pain helps us grow in our faith and our relationship with him (see Romans 5:3-5).

• **10:35-38** The Bible gives us a clear choice between two life directions. Because life often forks off in two directions, you must take the higher road, even though it looks more difficult and treacherous. That road gets steep in places. The climb takes a toll on your energy. It gets lonely. Not many are on it, but more than you imagined, and some because of your example. It gets slippery; the devil blows ice on the narrow passages. Despite its dangers, the higher road is bound for the peak, and you'll make it—God has a lifeline around you. When you are tempted to falter in your faith or to turn back from following Christ, keep focused on what he has done for you and what he offers in the future (see Romans 8:12-25; Galatians 3:10-13). Then keep climbing.

10:36 For the time being, these believers needed patient endurance, that is, to remain steadfast, to hold firm. Because Christ lives in us, we can have that kind of endurance. Jesus predicted that his followers would be severely persecuted by those who hated him (Matthew 10:22). In the midst of terrible persecution,

Great Examples of Faith

11:1
Rom 8:24
Heb 3:6, 14

11 Faith is the confidence that what we hope for will actually happen; it gives us assurance about things we cannot see. ²Through their faith, the people in days of old earned a good reputation.

11:3
Gen 1:1-31
Ps 33:6, 9
John 1:3
Rom 1:19-20
Heb 1:2

³By faith we understand that the entire universe was formed at God's command, that what we now see did not come from anything that can be seen.

11:4
Gen 4:3-10

⁴It was by faith that Abel brought a more acceptable offering to God than Cain did. Abel's offering gave evidence that he was a righteous man, and God showed his approval of his gifts. Although Abel is long dead, he still speaks to us by his example of faith.

11:5
Gen 5:22-24

⁵It was by faith that Enoch was taken up to heaven without dying—"he disappeared, because God took him."* For before he was taken up, he was known as a person who pleased God.

11:6
Heb 7:19

⁶And it is impossible to please God without faith. Anyone who wants to come to him must believe that God exists and that he rewards those who sincerely seek him.

11:7
Gen 6:13-22
Rom 3:22
1 Pet 3:20

⁷It was by faith that Noah built a large boat to save his family from the flood. He obeyed God, who warned him about things that had never happened before. By his faith Noah condemned the rest of the world, and he received the righteousness that comes by faith.

11:8
Gen 12:1-5
Acts 7:2-4

⁸It was by faith that Abraham obeyed when God called him to leave home and go to another land that God would give him as his inheritance. He went without knowing where he was going.

11:9
Gen 12:8

⁹And even when he reached the land God promised him, he lived there by faith—for he was like a foreigner, living in tents. And so did Isaac and Jacob, who inherited the same promise.

11:10
Heb 12:22
Rev 21:2

¹⁰Abraham was confidently looking forward to a city with eternal foundations, a city designed and built by God.

11:5 Gen 5:24.

---

they could have hope, however, knowing that salvation was theirs. Times of trial serve to sift true Christians from false or fair-weather Christians. When you are pressured to give up and turn your back on Christ, remember the benefits of standing firm and continue to live for Christ. Patient endurance is not a way to be saved but the evidence that you are really committed to Jesus.

11:1 Do you remember how you felt when you were very young and your birthday approached? You were excited and anxious. You knew you would certainly receive gifts and other special treats. But some things would be a surprise. Birthdays combine assurance and anticipation, and so does faith! Faith is the confidence based on past experience that God's new and fresh surprises will surely be ours.

• **11:1** The beginning point of faith is believing in God's character: He *is* who he says. The end point is believing in God's promises: He will *do* what he says. When we believe that God will fulfill his promises even though we don't see those promises materializing yet, we demonstrate true faith (see John 20:24-31).

• **11:3** God called the universe into existence out of nothing; he declared that it was to be, and it was. Our faith is in the God who created the entire universe by his word. God's word has awesome power. When he speaks, do you listen and respond? How can you better prepare yourself to respond to God's word?

11:4 Cain and Abel were Adam and Eve's first two sons. Abel offered a sacrifice that pleased God, while Cain's sacrifice was unacceptable. Abel's Profile is found in Genesis 5, p. 15. Cain's Profile is in Genesis 6, p. 17. Abel's sacrifice (an animal substitute) was more acceptable to God, both because it was a blood sacrifice and, most important, because of Abel's attitude when he offered it.

• **11:6** Believing that God exists is only the beginning; even the demons believe that much (James 2:19, 20). God will not settle for mere acknowledgment of his existence. He wants your faith that leads to a personal, dynamic relationship.

But does faith make sense, really? Do you believe because faith makes sense, or because faith doesn't need to make sense? Some Christians think people cannot understand God and should not try. Others believe that nothing true is irrational, including true faith. The truth is, God gave us minds that should be developed and used. To ignore intellectual growth is to live a stunted and naive life. God wants our trust and faith, even while we ponder and wonder about so many matters mysterious to us. Even so, we do not believe in a void nor leap into the dark. Faith is reasonable, though reason alone cannot explain the whole of it. So use your mind to think things through. But leave room for the unexplainable works of God.

11:6 Sometimes we wonder about the fate of those who haven't heard of Christ and have not even had a Bible to read. God assures us that all who honestly seek him—who act in faith on the knowledge of God that they possess—will be rewarded. When you tell others the Good News, encourage them to be honest and diligent in their search for truth. Those who hear the Good News are responsible for what they have heard (see 2 Corinthians 6:1, 2).

11:7 Noah experienced rejection because he was different from his neighbors. God commanded him to build a huge boat in the middle of dry land, and although God's command seemed foolish, Noah obeyed. Noah's obedience made him appear strange to his neighbors, just as the new beliefs of Jewish Christians undoubtedly made them stand out. As you obey God, don't be surprised if others regard you as "different." Your obedience makes their disobedience stand out. Remember, if God asks you to do something, he will give you the necessary strength to carry out that task. For more information on Noah, see his Profile in Genesis 8, p. 19.

11:8-10 Abraham's life was filled with faith. At God's command, he left home and went to another land—obeying without question (Genesis 12:1ff). He believed the covenant that God made with him (Genesis 12:2, 3; 13:14-16; 15:1-6). In obedience to God, Abraham was even willing to sacrifice his son Isaac (Genesis 22:1-19). Do not be surprised if God asks you to give up secure, familiar surroundings in order to carry out his will. For further information on Abraham, see his Profile in Genesis 18, p. 33.

¹¹It was by faith that even Sarah was able to have a child, though she was barren and was too old. She believed* that God would keep his promise. ¹²And so a whole nation came from this one man who was as good as dead—a nation with so many people that, like the stars in the sky and the sand on the seashore, there is no way to count them.

¹³All these people died still believing what God had promised them. They did not receive what was promised, but they saw it all from a distance and welcomed it. They agreed that they were foreigners and nomads here on earth. ¹⁴Obviously people who say such things are looking forward to a country they can call their own. ¹⁵If they had longed for the country they came from, they could have gone back. ¹⁶But they were looking for a better place, a heavenly homeland. That is why God is not ashamed to be called their God, for he has prepared a city for them.

¹⁷It was by faith that Abraham offered Isaac as a sacrifice when God was testing him. Abraham, who had received God's promises, was ready to sacrifice his only son, Isaac, ¹⁸even though God had told him, "Isaac is the son through whom your descendants will be counted."* ¹⁹Abraham reasoned that if Isaac died, God was able to bring him back to life again. And in a sense, Abraham did receive his son back from the dead.

²⁰It was by faith that Isaac promised blessings for the future to his sons, Jacob and Esau.

²¹It was by faith that Jacob, when he was old and dying, blessed each of Joseph's sons and bowed in worship as he leaned on his staff.

²²It was by faith that Joseph, when he was about to die, said confidently that the people of Israel would leave Egypt. He even commanded them to take his bones with them when they left.

²³It was by faith that Moses' parents hid him for three months when he was born. They saw that God had given them an unusual child, and they were not afraid to disobey the king's command.

11:11 Or *It was by faith that he [Abraham] was able to have a child, even though Sarah was barren and he was too old. He believed.* **11:18** Gen 21:12.

11:11
Gen 17:19; 21:1-3
11:12
Gen 15:5-6; 22:17
Rom 4:19
11:13
Gen 23:4
Matt 13:17
Heb 11:39
11:14
Heb 13:14
11:15
Gen 24:6-8
11:16
Gen 26:24
Exod 3:6, 15
11:17
Gen 22:1-10
Jas 2:21
11:18
†Gen 21:12
11:19
Rom 4:21
11:20
Gen 27:27-29
11:21
Gen 47:31;
48:15-16
11:22
Gen 50:24-25
Exod 13:19
11:23
Exod 1:16, 22; 2:2

11:11, 12 Sarah was Abraham's wife. They were unable to have children through many years of their marriage. God promised Abraham a son, but Sarah doubted that she could become pregnant in her old age. At first she laughed, but afterward, she believed (Genesis 18). For more information on Sarah, see her Profile in Genesis 19, p. 35.

11:13 That we are "foreigners and nomads" on earth may be an awareness forced on us by circumstances. It may come late in life or as the result of difficult times. But this world is not our home. We cannot live here forever (see also 1 Peter 1:1). It is best for us not to be so attached to this world's desires and possessions that we can't move out at God's command.

• **11:13-16** These people of faith died without receiving all that God had promised, but they never lost their vision of heaven ("a better place, a heavenly homeland"). Many Christians become frustrated and defeated because their needs, wants, expectations, and demands are not immediately met when they accept Christ as Savior. They become impatient and want to quit. Are you discouraged because the achievement of your goal seems far away? Take courage from these heroes of faith, who lived and died without seeing the fruit of their faith on earth and yet continued to believe (see 11:36-39).

11:17-19 Abraham was willing to give up his son when God commanded him to do so (Genesis 22:1-19). God did not let Abraham take Isaac's life, because God had given the command in order to test Abraham's faith. Instead of taking Abraham's son, God gave Abraham a whole nation of descendants through Isaac. If you are afraid to trust God with the possession, dream, or person you treasure most, pay attention to Abraham's example. Because Abraham was willing to give up everything for God, he received back more than he could have imagined. What we receive, however, is not always immediate or in the form of material possessions. Material things should be among the least satisfying of rewards. Our best and greatest rewards await us in eternity.

11:20 Isaac was the son who had been promised to Abraham and Sarah in their old age. It was through Isaac that God fulfilled his promise to eventually give Abraham countless descendants. Isaac had twin sons, Jacob and Esau. God chose the younger son, Jacob, through whom to continue the fulfillment of his promise to Abraham. For more information on Isaac, see his Profile in Genesis 19, p. 37.

11:21 Jacob was Isaac's son and Abraham's grandson. Jacob's sons became the fathers of Israel's 12 tribes. Even when Jacob (also called "Israel") was dying in a strange land, he believed the promise that Abraham's descendants would be like the sand on the seashore and that Israel would become a great nation (Genesis 48:1-22). True faith helps us see beyond the grave. For more information on Jacob and Esau, see their Profiles in Genesis 25, pp. 47 and 49.

11:22 Joseph, one of Jacob's sons, was sold into slavery by his jealous brothers (Genesis 37). Eventually, Joseph was sold again, this time to an official of the Pharaoh of Egypt. Because of Joseph's faithfulness to God, however, he was given a top-ranking position in Egypt. Although Joseph could have used that position to build a personal empire, he remembered God's promise to Abraham. After he had been reconciled to his brothers, Joseph brought his family to be near him and requested that his bones be taken to the Promised Land when the Jews eventually left Egypt (Genesis 50:24, 25). Faith means trusting in God and doing what he wants, regardless of the circumstances or consequences. For more information on Joseph, see his Profile in Genesis 37, p. 71.

11:23 Moses' parents trusted God to protect their son's life. They were not merely proud parents; they were believers who had faith that God would care for him. As a parent, have you trusted God enough to take care of your children? God has a plan for every person, and your important task is to pray for your children and prepare them to do the work God has planned for them to do. Faith allows us to entrust even our children to God.

11:24
Exod 2:10-12

11:26
Heb 13:13

11:27
Exod 12:50-51

11:28
Exod 12:21-30

11:29
Exod 14:21-31

11:30
Josh 6:12-21

11:31
Josh 2:11-12;
6:20-25
Jas 2:25

11:32
Judg 4–13
1 Sam 1:20;
16:1, 13

11:33
1 Sam 17:34-36
Dan 6:1-27

11:34
2 Kgs 20:7
Dan 3:19-27

11:35
1 Kgs 17:17-24
2 Kgs 4:25-37

11:36
Gen 39:20
Jer 20:2; 37:15

11:37
1 Kgs 19:10
2 Chr 24:20-22

11:38
1 Kgs 18:4; 19:9

24It was by faith that Moses, when he grew up, refused to be called the son of Pharaoh's daughter. 25He chose to share the oppression of God's people instead of enjoying the fleeting pleasures of sin. 26He thought it was better to suffer for the sake of Christ than to own the treasures of Egypt, for he was looking ahead to his great reward. 27It was by faith that Moses left the land of Egypt, not fearing the king's anger. He kept right on going because he kept his eyes on the one who is invisible. 28It was by faith that Moses commanded the people of Israel to keep the Passover and to sprinkle blood on the doorposts so that the angel of death would not kill their firstborn sons.

29It was by faith that the people of Israel went right through the Red Sea as though they were on dry ground. But when the Egyptians tried to follow, they were all drowned.

30It was by faith that the people of Israel marched around Jericho for seven days, and the walls came crashing down.

31It was by faith that Rahab the prostitute was not destroyed with the people in her city who refused to obey God. For she had given a friendly welcome to the spies.

32How much more do I need to say? It would take too long to recount the stories of the faith of Gideon, Barak, Samson, Jephthah, David, Samuel, and all the prophets. 33By faith these people overthrew kingdoms, ruled with justice, and received what God had promised them. They shut the mouths of lions, 34quenched the flames of fire, and escaped death by the edge of the sword. Their weakness was turned to strength. They became strong in battle and put whole armies to flight. 35Women received their loved ones back again from death.

But others were tortured, refusing to turn from God in order to be set free. They placed their hope in a better life after the resurrection. 36Some were jeered at, and their backs were cut open with whips. Others were chained in prisons. 37Some died by stoning, some were sawed in half,* and others were killed with the sword. Some went about wearing skins of sheep and goats, destitute and oppressed and mistreated. 38They were too good for this world, wandering over deserts and mountains, hiding in caves and holes in the ground.

11:37 Some manuscripts add *some were tested.*

11:24-28 Moses became one of Israel's greatest leaders, a prophet and a lawgiver. But when he was born, his people were slaves in Egypt, and the Egyptian officials had ordered that all Hebrew baby boys were to be killed. Moses was spared, however, and Pharaoh's daughter raised Moses in Pharaoh's own household (Exodus 1–2)! It took faith for Moses to give up his place in the palace, but he could do it because he saw the fleeting nature of great wealth and prestige. It is easy to be deceived by the temporary benefits of wealth, popularity, status, and achievement, and to be blind to the long-range benefits of God's Kingdom. Faith helps us look beyond the world's value system to see the eternal values of God's Kingdom. For more information on Moses, see his Profile in Exodus 14, p. 117.

11:26 True wealth is eternal. Consider the most powerful or well-known people in our world—how many got where they are by being humble, self-effacing, and gentle? Not many! But in the life to come, the last will be first—if they got in last place by choosing to follow Jesus. Hebrews has a critical message for earth-loving Christians. Don't forfeit eternal rewards for temporary benefits. Like Moses, be willing to make sacrifices now for greater rewards later (Matthew 6:19-21).

11:31 When Joshua planned the conquest of Jericho, he sent spies to investigate the fortifications of the city. The spies met Rahab, who had two strikes against her—she was a Gentile and a prostitute. But she showed that she had faith in God by welcoming the spies and by trusting God to spare her and her family when the city was destroyed. Faith helps us turn around and do what is right regardless of our past or the disapproval of others. For more information on Rahab, see her Profile in Joshua 6, p. 321.

• **11:32-35** The Old Testament records the lives of the various people who experienced these great victories. Joshua and Deborah overthrew kingdoms (the book of Joshua; Judges 4–5). Nehemiah ruled with justice (the book of Nehemiah). Daniel was saved from the mouths of lions (Daniel 6). Shadrach, Meshach, and Abednego were kept from harm in the flames of a blazing furnace (Daniel 3). Elijah escaped the edge of the swords of evil Queen Jezebel's

henchmen (1 Kings 19:2ff). Hezekiah regained strength after sickness (2 Kings 20). Gideon was strong in battle (Judges 7). A widow's son was brought back to life by the prophet Elisha (2 Kings 4:8-37).

We, too, can experience victory through faith in Christ. Our victories over oppressors may be like those of the Old Testament saints, but more likely, our victories will be directly related to the role God wants us to play. Even though our body deteriorates and dies, we will live forever because of Christ. In the promised resurrection, even death will be defeated, and Christ's victory will be made complete.

• **11:32-40** These verses summarize the lives of other great men and women of faith. Some experienced outstanding victories, even over the threat of death. But others were severely mistreated, tortured, and even killed. Having a steadfast faith in God does not guarantee a happy, carefree life. On the contrary, our faith almost guarantees us some form of abuse from the world. While we are on earth, we may never see the purpose of our suffering. But we know that God will keep his promises to us. Do you believe that God will keep his promises to you?

• **11:35-39** Many think that pain is the exception in the Christian life. When suffering occurs, they say, "Why me?" They feel as though God deserted them, or perhaps they accuse him of not being as dependable as they thought. In reality, however, we live in an evil world filled with suffering, even for believers. But God is still in control. He allows some Christians to become martyrs for the faith, and he allows others to survive persecution. Rather than asking, "Why me?" it is much more helpful to ask, "Why not me?" Our faith and the values of this world are on a collision course. If we expect pain and suffering to come, we will not be shocked when they hit. But we can also take comfort in knowing that Jesus also suffered. He understands our fears, our weaknesses, and our disappointments (see 2:16-18; 4:14-16). He promised never to leave us (Matthew 28:18-20), and he intercedes on our behalf (7:24, 25). In times of pain, persecution, or suffering, we should trust confidently in Christ.

39All these people earned a good reputation because of their faith, yet none of them received all that God had promised. 40For God had something better in mind for us, so that they would not reach perfection without us.

11:40
Rom 11:26
Rev 6:11

God's Discipline Proves His Love

12 Therefore, since we are surrounded by such a huge crowd of witnesses to the life of faith, let us strip off every weight that slows us down, especially the sin that so easily trips us up. And let us run with endurance the race God has set before us. 2We do this by keeping our eyes on Jesus, the champion who initiates and perfects our faith.* Because of the joy* awaiting him, he endured the cross, disregarding its shame. Now he is seated in the place of honor beside God's throne. 3Think of all the hostility he endured from sinful people;* then you won't become weary and give up. 4After all, you have not yet given your lives in your struggle against sin.

12:1
1 Cor 9:24
Phil 3:12-14

12:2
Ps 110:1
Phil 2:8-9
Heb 2:9-10
1 Pet 1:11

12:4
Heb 10:32-34

5And have you forgotten the encouraging words God spoke to you as his children?* He said,

12:5-6
†Prov 3:11-12

"My child,* don't make light of the LORD's discipline,
    and don't give up when he corrects you.
6 For the LORD disciplines those he loves,
    and he punishes each one he accepts as his child."*

12:6
Rev 3:19

7As you endure this divine discipline, remember that God is treating you as his own children. Who ever heard of a child who is never disciplined by its father? 8If God doesn't discipline you as he does all of his children, it means that you are illegitimate and are not really his children at all. 9Since we respected our earthly fathers who disciplined us, shouldn't we submit even more to the discipline of the Father of our spirits, and live forever?*

12:7
Deut 8:5
2 Sam 7:14

12:8
1 Pet 5:9

12:9
Isa 38:16

10For our earthly fathers disciplined us for a few years, doing the best they knew how. But God's discipline is always good for us, so that we might share in his holiness. 11No discipline is enjoyable while it is happening—it's painful! But afterward there will be a peaceful harvest of right living for those who are trained in this way.

12:10
2 Pet 1:4

12:11
Jas 3:17-18

12:2a Or *Jesus, the originator and perfecter of our faith.*   **12:2b** Or *Instead of the joy.*   **12:3** Some manuscripts read *Think of how people hurt themselves by opposing him.*   **12:5a** Greek *sons;* also in 12:7, 8.   **12:5b** Greek *son;* also in 12:6, 7.   **12:5-6** Prov 3:11-12 (Greek version).   **12:9** Or *and really live?*

• **11:39, 40** Hebrews 11 has been called faith's hall of fame. No doubt the author surprised his readers by this conclusion: These mighty Jewish heroes did not receive all that God had promised because they died before Christ came. In God's plan, they and the Christian believers (who were also enduring much testing) would be rewarded together. Once again Hebrews shows that Christianity offers a better way than Judaism.

11:40 There is a solidarity among believers (see 12:23). Old and New Testament believers will be glorified together. Not only are we one in the body of Christ with all those alive, but we are also one with all those who ever lived. It takes all of us to be perfect in him.

• **12:1** This "huge crowd of witnesses" is composed of the people described in chapter 11. Their faithfulness is a constant encouragement to us. We do not struggle alone, and we are not the first to struggle with the problems we face. Others have run the race and won, and their witness stirs us to run and win also. What an inspiring heritage we have!

12:1 Long-distance runners work hard to build endurance and strength. On race day, their clothes are lightweight and their bodies lean. To run the race that God has set before us, we must also strip off the excess weight that slows us down. How can we do that? (1) Choose friends who are also committed to the race. Wrong friends will have values and activities that may deter you from the course. Much of your own weight may result from the crowd you run with. Make wise choices. (2) Drop certain activities. That is, for you at this time these may be weight. Try dropping them for a while; then check the results in your life. (3) Get help for addictions that disable you. If you have a secret "weight" such as pornography, gambling, or alcohol, admit your need and get help today.

• **12:1-4** The Christian life involves hard work. It requires us to give up whatever endangers our relationship with God, to run with endurance, and to struggle against sin with the power of the Holy Spirit. To live effectively, we must keep our eyes on Jesus. We will stumble if we look away from him to stare at ourselves or at the circumstances surrounding us. We should be running for Christ, not ourselves, and we must always keep him in sight.

• **12:3** When we face hardship and discouragement, it is easy to lose sight of the big picture. But we're not alone; there is help. Many have already made it through life, enduring far more difficult circumstances than we have experienced. Suffering is the training ground for Christian maturity. It develops our patience and makes our final victory sweet.

• **12:4** These readers were facing difficult times of persecution, but none of them had yet died for their faith. Because they were still alive, the writer urged them to continue to run their race. Just as Christ did not give up, neither should they.

• **12:5-11** Who loves his child more—the father who allows the child to do what will harm him, or the one who corrects, trains, and even punishes the child to help him learn what is right? It's never pleasant to be corrected and disciplined by God, but his discipline is a sign of his deep love for us. When God corrects you, see it as proof of his love, and ask him what he is trying to teach you.

• **12:11** We may respond to discipline in several ways: (1) We can accept it with resignation; (2) we can accept it with self-pity, thinking we really don't deserve it; (3) we can be angry and resentful toward God; or (4) we can accept it gratefully, as the appropriate response we owe a loving Father.

12:12
Isa 35:3

12:13
Prov 4:26

¹²So take a new grip with your tired hands and strengthen your weak knees. ¹³Mark out a straight path for your feet so that those who are weak and lame will not fall but become strong.

A Call to Listen to God

12:14
Rom 14:19

12:15
Deut 29:17-18
Heb 4:1

12:16
Gen 25:29-34

12:17
Gen 27:30-40

¹⁴Work at living in peace with everyone, and work at living a holy life, for those who are not holy will not see the Lord. ¹⁵Look after each other so that none of you fails to receive the grace of God. Watch out that no poisonous root of bitterness grows up to trouble you, corrupting many. ¹⁶Make sure that no one is immoral or godless like Esau, who traded his birthright as the firstborn son for a single meal. ¹⁷You know that afterward, when he wanted his father's blessing, he was rejected. It was too late for repentance, even though he begged with bitter tears.

12:18-19
Exod 19:16-22;
20:18-21
Deut 4:11-12;
5:22-27

12:20
†Exod 19:12-13

12:21
Deut 9:19

¹⁸You have not come to a physical mountain,* to a place of flaming fire, darkness, gloom, and whirlwind, as the Israelites did at Mount Sinai. ¹⁹For they heard an awesome trumpet blast and a voice so terrible that they begged God to stop speaking. ²⁰They staggered back under God's command: "If even an animal touches the mountain, it must be stoned to death."* ²¹Moses himself was so frightened at the sight that he said, "I am terrified and trembling."*

12:22
Gal 4:26
Rev 5:11; 21:2

12:23
Gen 18:25
Phil 3:12

12:24
Gen 4:10
Heb 9:19; 10:22

²²No, you have come to Mount Zion, to the city of the living God, the heavenly Jerusalem, and to countless thousands of angels in a joyful gathering. ²³You have come to the assembly of God's firstborn children, whose names are written in heaven. You have come to God himself, who is the judge over all things. You have come to the spirits of the righteous ones in heaven who have now been made perfect. ²⁴You have come to Jesus, the one who mediates the new covenant between God and people, and to the sprinkled blood, which speaks of forgiveness instead of crying out for vengeance like the blood of Abel.

12:25
Heb 2:1-3;
10:28-29

12:26
Exod 19:18
†Hag 2:6

12:27
2 Pet 3:10

²⁵Be careful that you do not refuse to listen to the One who is speaking. For if the people of Israel did not escape when they refused to listen to Moses, the earthly messenger, we will certainly not escape if we reject the One who speaks to us from heaven! ²⁶When God spoke from Mount Sinai his voice shook the earth, but now he makes another promise: "Once again I will shake not only the earth but the heavens also."* ²⁷This means that all of creation will be shaken and removed, so that only unshakable things will remain.

12:18 Greek *to something that can be touched.*   **12:20** Exod 19:13.   **12:21** Deut 9:19.   **12:26** Hag 2:6.

• **12:12, 13** God is not only a disciplining parent but also a demanding coach who pushes us to our limits and requires our lives to be disciplined. Although we may not feel strong enough to push on to victory, we will be able to accomplish it as we follow Christ and draw on his strength. Then we can use our growing strength to help those around us who are weak and struggling.

12:12, 13 We must not live with only our own survival in mind. Others will follow our example, and we have a responsibility to them if we are living for Christ, as we claim to be. Does your example make it easier for others to believe in and follow Christ, and to mature in him? Or would those who follow you end up confused and misled?

12:14 The readers were familiar with the ceremonial cleansing ritual that prepared them for worship, and they knew that they had to be holy or clean in order to enter the Temple. Sin always blocks our vision of God; so if we want to see God, we must renounce sin and obey him (see Psalm 24:3, 4). Holiness is coupled with living in peace. A right relationship with God leads to right relationships with fellow believers. Although we will not always feel loving toward all other believers, we must pursue peace as we become more Christlike.

12:15 Like a small root that grows into a great tree, bitterness springs up in our hearts and overshadows even our deepest Christian relationships. A "poisonous root of bitterness" comes when we allow disappointment to grow into resentment, or when we nurse grudges over past hurts. Bitterness brings with it jealousy, dissension, and immorality. When the Holy Spirit fills us, however, he can heal the hurt that causes bitterness.

12:16, 17 Esau's story shows us that mistakes and sins sometimes have lasting consequences (Genesis 25:29-34; 27:36). Even

repentance and forgiveness do not always eliminate sin's consequences. How often do you make decisions based on what you want now, rather than on what you need in the long run? Evaluate the long-range effects of your decisions and actions.

12:18-24 What a contrast between the people's terrified approach to God at Mount Sinai and their joyful approach at Mount Zion! What a difference Jesus has made! Before Jesus came, God seemed distant and threatening. After Jesus came, God welcomes us through Christ into his presence. Accept God's invitation!

12:22 As Christians, we are citizens of the heavenly Jerusalem right now; because Christ rules our lives, the Holy Spirit is always with us, and we experience close fellowship with other believers. The full and ultimate rewards and reality of the heavenly Jerusalem are depicted in Revelation 21.

12:27-29 Eventually the world will crumble, and only God's Kingdom will last. Those who follow Christ are part of this unshakable Kingdom, and they will withstand the shaking, sifting, and burning. When we feel unsure about the future, we can take confidence from these verses. No matter what happens here, our future is built on a solid foundation that cannot be destroyed. Don't put your confidence in what will be destroyed; instead, build your life on Christ and his unshakable Kingdom. (See Matthew 7:24-27 for the importance of building on a solid foundation.)

²⁸Since we are receiving a Kingdom that is unshakable, let us be thankful and please God by worshiping him with holy fear and awe. ²⁹For our God is a devouring fire.

12:28
Dan 2:44

Concluding Words

13 Keep on loving each other as brothers and sisters.* ²Don't forget to show hospitality to strangers, for some who have done this have entertained angels without realizing it! ³Remember those in prison, as if you were there yourself. Remember also those being mistreated, as if you felt their pain in your own bodies.

⁴Give honor to marriage, and remain faithful to one another in marriage. God will surely judge people who are immoral and those who commit adultery.

⁵Don't love money; be satisfied with what you have. For God has said,

"I will never fail you.
   I will never abandon you."*

⁶So we can say with confidence,

"The LORD is my helper,
   so I will have no fear.
What can mere people do to me?"*

⁷Remember your leaders who taught you the word of God. Think of all the good that has come from their lives, and follow the example of their faith.

13:1
Rom 12:10

13:2
Gen 18:1-8; 19:1-3

13:3
Matt 25:36
Col 4:18
Heb 10:34

13:4
1 Cor 7:38

13:5
Gen 28:15
†Deut 31:5
Josh 1:5

13:6
†Ps 118:6

13:7
Heb 6:12

13:1 Greek *Continue in brotherly love.*   **13:5** Deut 31:6, 8.   **13:6** Ps 118:6.

12:28 Here are five ways we can be thankful: (1) We can be thankful that God answers our prayers (Isaiah 65:24; John 11:41). (2) We can be thankful for God's provision for our needs (1 Thessalonians 5:17, 18; 1 Timothy 4:4, 5). (3) We can be thankful for God's blessings (1 Chronicles 16:34; Philippians 4:6). (4) We can be thankful for God's character and wondrous works (Psalm 7:17; 2 Corinthians 9:15; Revelation 11:17). (5) We can be thankful for our brothers and sisters in Christ (1 Corinthians 1:4; Ephesians 1:16; Philippians 1:3-5).

12:29 There is a big difference between the flame of a candle and the roaring blast of a forest fire. We cannot even stand near a raging fire. Even with sophisticated firefighting equipment, a devouring fire is often beyond human control. God is not within our control either. We cannot force him to do anything for us through our prayers. He cannot be contained. Yet, he is a God of compassion. He has saved us from sin, and he will save us from death. But everything that is worthless and sinful will be devoured by the fire of his wrath. Only what is good, dedicated to God, and righteous will remain.

• **13:1-5** Real love for others produces tangible actions: (1) hospitality to strangers (13:2); (2) empathy for those who are in prison and those who have been mistreated (13:3); (3) respect for your marriage vows (13:4); and (4) contentment with what you have (13:5). Make sure that your love runs deep enough to affect your hospitality, empathy, fidelity, and contentment.

• **13:2** Three Old Testament people "entertained angels without realizing it": (1) Abraham (Genesis 18:1ff), (2) Gideon (Judges 6:11ff), and (3) Manoah (Judges 13:2ff). Some people say they cannot be hospitable because their homes are not large enough or nice enough. But even if you have no more than a table and two chairs in a rented room, there are people who would be grateful to spend time in your home. Are there visitors to your church with whom you could share a meal? Do you know single people who would enjoy an evening of conversation? Is there any way your home could meet the needs of traveling missionaries? Hospitality simply means making other people feel comfortable and at home.

• **13:3** We are to have empathy for those in prison, especially for (but not limited to) Christians imprisoned for their faith. Jesus said that his true followers would represent him as they visit those in prison (Matthew 25:36). Prisons are a mission field—believers can send in evangelists and Bible teachers. Prison systems are political projects—Christian voices are needed regarding justice and mercy in funding, staff training, and rehabilitative programs. Prisons are an international problem—through multi-national Christian agencies, believers can help victims in other countries. Compassion for suffering people demands no less. There is a wide open field of ways to obey this command to "remember those in prison."

13:4 Giving honor to marriage will require the utmost in Christian conviction and sensitivity. Modern social theory may redefine the family, and the new definitions may be far from its biblical foundation. What can you do? Witness to the depth of God's love for you by keeping your marriage happy and strong. Remain faithful—in body and in mind. Pray for your spouse. Honor biblical marriage (consenting man-woman unions) by resisting political pressure to recognize and legalize other sexual preferences. Teach children the biblical meaning of marriage. Pray early for their own eventual spouses and families. Make marriage enrichment the goal of your small group discussions and study. Encourage the marriages around you to stay strong as well.

• **13:5, 6** How can we learn to be satisfied with what we have? Strive to live with less rather than desiring more; give away out of your abundance rather than accumulating more; relish what you have rather than resent what you're missing. We become satisfied when we realize God's sufficiency for our needs. Christians who become materialistic are saying by their actions that God can't take care of them—or at least that he won't take care of them the way they want. Insecurity can lead to the love of money, whether we are rich or poor. The only antidote is to trust God to meet all our needs. See God's love expressed in what he has provided, and remember that money and possessions will all pass away. (See Philippians 4:11 for more on contentment, and 1 John 2:17 for the futility of earthly desires.)

• **13:7** If you are a Christian, you owe much to others who have taught you and modeled for you what you needed to know about the Good News and Christian living. Continue following the good examples of those who have invested themselves in you by investing in your life through evangelism, service, and Christian education.

13:8
Heb 1:12

13:9
Eph 4:14
Col 2:7, 16

13:11
Lev 4:12, 21; 16:27

13:12
John 19:17
Heb 9:12

13:13
Heb 11:26

13:14
Heb 11:10; 12:22

13:15
Ps 50:14
Hos 14:2
1 Pet 2:5

13:16
Phil 4:18

13:17
Isa 62:6
Ezek 3:17
Acts 20:28

13:19
Phlm 1:22

13:20
Isa 55:3
Jer 32:40; 50:5
Ezek 37:26
Zech 9:11
John 10:11

13:21
Rom 11:36
Phil 2:13

8Jesus Christ is the same yesterday, today, and forever. 9So do not be attracted by strange, new ideas. Your strength comes from God's grace, not from rules about food, which don't help those who follow them.

10We have an altar from which the priests in the Tabernacle* have no right to eat. 11Under the old system, the high priest brought the blood of animals into the Holy Place as a sacrifice for sin, and the bodies of the animals were burned outside the camp. 12So also Jesus suffered and died outside the city gates to make his people holy by means of his own blood. 13So let us go out to him, outside the camp, and bear the disgrace he bore. 14For this world is not our permanent home; we are looking forward to a home yet to come.

15Therefore, let us offer through Jesus a continual sacrifice of praise to God, proclaiming our allegiance to his name. 16And don't forget to do good and to share with those in need. These are the sacrifices that please God.

17Obey your spiritual leaders, and do what they say. Their work is to watch over your souls, and they are accountable to God. Give them reason to do this with joy and not with sorrow. That would certainly not be for your benefit.

18Pray for us, for our conscience is clear and we want to live honorably in everything we do. 19And especially pray that I will be able to come back to you soon.

20 Now may the God of peace—
    who brought up from the dead our Lord Jesus,
  the great Shepherd of the sheep,
    and ratified an eternal covenant with his blood—
21 may he equip you with all you need
    for doing his will.
  May he produce in you,*
    through the power of Jesus Christ,

13:10 Or *tent.*   13:21 Some manuscripts read *in us.*

• **13:8** Though human leaders have much to offer, we must keep our eyes on Christ, our ultimate leader. Unlike any human leaders, he will never change. Christ has been and will be the same forever. In a changing world we can trust our unchanging Lord.

13:9 Apparently some were teaching that keeping the Old Testament ceremonial laws and rituals (such as not eating certain foods) was important for salvation. But these laws were useless for conquering a person's evil thoughts and desires (Colossians 2:23). The laws could influence conduct, but they could not change the heart. Lasting changes in conduct begin when the Holy Spirit lives in each person.

13:13 The Jewish Christians were being ridiculed and persecuted by Jews who didn't believe in Jesus the Messiah. Most of the book of Hebrews tells them how Christ is greater than the sacrificial system. Here the writer drives home the point of his lengthy argument: It may be necessary to leave the "camp" and suffer with Christ. To be outside the camp meant to be unclean—in the days of the Exodus, those who were ceremonially unclean had to stay outside the camp. But Jesus suffered humiliation and uncleanness outside the Jerusalem gates on their behalf. The time had come for Jewish Christians to declare their loyalty to Christ above any other loyalty, to choose to follow the Messiah whatever suffering that might entail. They needed to move outside the safe confinement of their past, their traditions, and their ceremonies to live for Christ. What holds you back from complete loyalty to Jesus Christ?

• **13:14** Christians love their families, spouses, jobs, and churches—but their sights should be set ahead beyond the horizon. Christians are activists, invested in witnessing to a needy world—but they take frequent glances toward a promised community still to come. Christians are gardeners and builders, shaping environments, turning weed pits into floral splendor, painting and patching and clearing—but they know God is building something far more beautiful and breathtaking just for them. Christians should be characterized by looking forward to the future. We should not be attached to this world, because all that we are and have here is temporary. We should not love our pres-

ent home so much that we lose sight of God's future blessing. Don't store up your treasures here; store them in heaven (Matthew 6:19-21).

13:15 Our lips should confess God's name in praise. Yet, in your typical day, how many times do you hear God's name used profanely? Christians should turn their frequency toward praise! Praise God early in the day before the rush, then again in the hurried middle, and at the end as business winds down. Offer Jesus a continual sacrifice of praise.

13:15, 16 Since these Jewish Christians, because of their witness to the Messiah, no longer worshiped with other Jews, they should consider praise and acts of service their sacrifices—ones they could offer anywhere, anytime. This must have reminded them of the prophet Hosea's words, "Forgive all our sins and graciously receive us, so that we may offer you our praises" (Hosea 14:2). A "sacrifice of praise" today would include thanking Christ for his sacrifice on the cross and telling others about it. Acts of kindness and sharing are particularly pleasing to God, even when they go unnoticed by others.

• **13:17** The task of church leaders is to help people mature in Christ. Cooperative followers greatly ease the burden of leadership. Does your conduct give your leaders reason to report joyfully about you?

• **13:18, 19** The writer recognizes the need for prayer. Christian leaders are especially vulnerable to criticism from others, pride (if they succeed), depression (if they fail), and Satan's constant efforts to destroy their work for God. The leaders in your church have been placed in that position by a loving God who has entrusted them with the responsibility of caring for you. Your leaders need your prayers! For whom should you regularly pray?

• **13:20, 21** These verses include two significant results of Christ's death and resurrection. God works in us to make us the kind of people that would please him, and he equips us to do the kind of *work* that would please him. Let God change you from within and then use you to help others.

every good thing that is pleasing to him.

All glory to him forever and ever! Amen.

²²I urge you, dear brothers and sisters,* to pay attention to what I have written in this brief exhortation.

²³I want you to know that our brother Timothy has been released from jail. If he comes here soon, I will bring him with me to see you.

²⁴Greet all your leaders and all the believers there.* The believers from Italy send you their greetings.

²⁵May God's grace be with you all.

13:22 1 Pet 5:12

13:23 Acts 16:1

13:22 Greek *brothers.*   **13:24** Greek *all of God's holy people.*

13:23 We have no record of Timothy's imprisonment, but we know that he had been in prison because it states here that he had been released. For more about Timothy, see his Profile in 1 Timothy 2, p. 2059.

13:24, 25 Hebrews is a call to Christian maturity. It was addressed to first-century Jewish Christians, but it applies to Christians of any age or background. Christian maturity means making Christ the beginning and end of our faith. To grow in maturity, we must center our life on him, not depending on religious ritual, not falling back into sin, not trusting in ourselves, and not letting anything come between us and Christ. Christ is sufficient and superior.

STUDY QUESTIONS

Thirteen lessons for individual or group study

It's always exciting to get more than you expect. And that's what you'll find in this Bible study guide—much more than you expect. Our goal was to write thoughtful, practical, dependable, and application-oriented studies of God's word.

This study guide contains the complete text of the selected Bible book. The commentary is accurate, complete, and loaded with unique charts, maps, and profiles of Bible people.

With the Bible text, extensive notes and helps, and questions to guide discussion, *Life Application Bible Studies* have everything you need in one place.

The lessons in this Bible study guide will work for large classes as well as small-group studies. To get everyone involved in your discussions, encourage participants to answer the questions before each meeting.

Each lesson is divided into five easy-to-lead sections. The section called "Reflect" introduces you and the members of your group to a specific area of life touched by the lesson. "Read" shows which chapters to read and which notes and other features to use. Additional questions help you understand the passage. "Realize" brings into focus the biblical principle to be learned with questions, a special insight, or both. "Respond" helps you make connections with your own situation and personal needs. The questions are designed to help you find areas in your life where you can apply the biblical truths. "Resolve" helps you map out action plans for that day.

Begin and end each lesson with prayer, asking for the Holy Spirit's guidance, direction, and wisdom.

Recommended time allotments for each section of a lesson are as follows:

Segment	60 minutes	90 minutes
Reflect on your life	*5 minutes*	*10 minutes*
Read the passage	*10 minutes*	*15 minutes*
Realize the principle	*15 minutes*	*20 minutes*
Respond to the message	*20 minutes*	*30 minutes*
Resolve to take action	*10 minutes*	*15 minutes*

All five sections work together to help a person learn the lessons, live out the principles, and obey the commands taught in the Bible.

Also, at the end of each lesson, there is a section entitled "More for studying other themes in this section." These questions will help you lead the group in studying other parts of each section not covered in depth by the main lesson.

But don't just listen to God's word. You must do what it says. Otherwise, you are only fooling yourselves. For if you listen to the word and don't obey, it is like glancing at your face in a mirror. You see yourself, walk away, and forget what you look like. But if you look carefully into the perfect law that sets you free, and if you do what it says and don't forget what you heard, then God will bless you for doing it (James 1:22-25).

LESSON 1
GOD'S BEST!
HEBREWS INTRODUCTION

R
REFLECT
on your life

1 Outside of your family, which people had the greatest positive influence on your childhood? *(age 10 r/12*

Grandma Barret.

2 Describe one way their influence has lasted in your life.

Respect to parents + Elders

R
READ
the passage

Read the introduction to Hebrews, Hebrews 1:1-3, and the following notes:

❏ 1:1   ❏ 1:1, 2   ❏ 1:3

3 What factors made it difficult for devout Jews to accept Jesus as their Messiah (see Introduction)?

His death, lack of physical king / No kingdom,

4 In what ways do people settle for less than Christ (see Introduction)?

_____

_____

_____

5 Who is Jesus and what did he do (1:1-3)?

God's Son, created all things, died for our sin + arose from the grave + lives in our hearts,

When the book of Hebrews was written, many people were questioning Jesus' identity as God's Son. The author wanted to reassure Jewish believers that Jesus was the perfect revelation of God, the perfect sacrifice for sin, and the only intermediary they needed before God. Christ is better than the old system of sacrifices and forgiveness that many wanted to resume. Nothing—no system and no person—can take Jesus' place. Jesus' identity and qualifications are still questioned today. It doesn't matter what people say about Jesus. The truth stands—he is the God-man and our only hope for eternal life. "Jesus Christ is the same yesterday, today, and forever" (13:8).

REALIZE
the principle

6 In what ways is Jesus superior to the old system of sacrifices and priests?

He is God, creator + sustainer of all Holy, pure, perfic,

7 What wrong ideas do people have about Jesus today?

he was created, his life was not enough,

_____

_____

8 What are some reasons people give for rejecting Christ?

_____

_____

_____

_____

9 How does the book of Hebrews answer objections to following Christ?

_____

_____

_____

_____

_____

RESPOND
to the message

10 Hebrews says that Jesus is superior to the old system of priests and sacrifices. What is Jesus superior to today?

He is Lord + lord + King of kings

Nothing before Or above Him

_____

_____

11 Why is Jesus' superiority important to the way we live?

He is all truth for all things + all times

_____

_____

_____

12 What situations might cause you to doubt the superiority of Christ?

_____

_____

_____

_____

_____

13 How can a correct understanding of his superiority help you live by faith each day?

_____

_____

_____

_____

14 Read the first paragraph of "The Blueprint" section, and check the box that best represents your present level of commitment to the point of view of Hebrews:

☑ Convinced of the superiority of Christ

☑ Growing confident of the superiority of Christ

☐ Seeking understanding of the superiority of Christ

☐ Have many questions about the superiority of Christ

☐ Have many doubts about the superiority of Christ

☐ Unconvinced of the superiority of Christ

15 What kind of influence do you want Christ to have in your life?

Complete

RESOLVE
to take action

16 As you study Hebrews, ask God to give you a deeper appreciation for Jesus Christ.

A What does the book of Hebrews contribute to the New Testament? How does it challenge you in ways that other books do not?

MORE
for studying
other themes
in this section

B Is it easier to keep the faith when you are harassed for it or when you receive a lot of support for it? What steps can you take to strengthen your faith?

C Given the writing style and subject matter of Hebrews, who would you think wrote this book? How does the author's identity affect your understanding of the book?

D Which of the last three "Megathemes" (Maturity, Faith, Endurance) would you most like to see grow in your life as a result of this study? Why?

Heb, the Book of better things Pg 11 second paragraph.

LESSON 2
NO ESCAPE
HEBREWS 1:1–2:4

R

REFLECT
on your life

1 What are some undeniable facts about you?

Mas F Heart, where you live, work, age

2 What are some undeniable facts about Christ?

God's Son, Messiah, lived, died, arose, olive day,
coming age.

How many people would listen if an angel of God spoke
without we here to Word complete?
I Cor 2:4 "in demonstration of the Spirit + of power."

Read Hebrews 1:1–2:4 and the following notes:

☐ 1:1, 2   ☐ 1:3   ☐ 1:4   ☐ 1:4ff   ☐ 1:11, 12   ☐ 1:14

R

READ
the passage

3 This passage explains that Jesus is greater than the angels. Why were angels so revered at that time?

They were taught that they interceded for people.

4 What are the differences between Jesus and the angels (1:1-14)? In what ways is Jesus greater than the angels?

Above the angles, responsibility for judgment.

5 In what ways is Jesus superior to creation (1:10-12)?

He created all things, sustains all things.

The readers of the book of Hebrews were fascinated with angels, seeing them as mediators between people and God. The author let them know that Jesus is far greater than the angels and the only way to God. People today also look for alternatives to Jesus. But the Bible makes it clear that there is only one way (John 14:6; Acts 4:12). If we ignore God's way of salvation, there is no escape from the eternal consequences.

REALIZE
the principle

6 What happens to people who ignore God's way of salvation?

Die in their sins, condemned!

7 What would you say to someone who says, "It doesn't matter what you believe as long as you're sincere"?

Wrong, The Word says that Jesus is the only way.

RESPOND
to the message

8 What are some ways people try to find God or gain eternal life?

Works,

9 How should the truth that Jesus Christ is the only way affect the way Christians live?

To live in obedience to God by keeping his word.
Put away any false teaching.

10 How should the truth that Jesus Christ is the only way affect how Christians interact with unbelievers?

To live a obedient example of Christ used in
them.

11 Think of a recent interaction you have had with another person. How did your faith affect that interaction?

12 Whom should you talk to about the fact that salvation can be found only in Christ?

Any none believer Christians that are questing their faith

RESOLVE
to take action

13 What is the first step you can take to give that person this message?

MORE
for studying
other themes
in this section

A Before Christ came, how did God communicate with people (1:1)? How does he communicate today (1:1-3)? What has he communicated to you that has changed your life?

B What has Christ done with our sins (1:3)? How does this truth affect your life?

C Other than Christ, who or what do people tend to depend on for security (1:10-12)? What practical difference does it make in your life that Christ never changes (1:12)?

D Who are angels (1:5-14)? What can you learn from their behavior?

LESSON 3
MAN ALIVE!
HEBREWS 2:5-18

REFLECT
on your life

1 What do people usually mean when they say, "I'm only human"?

Limited in strength or what is over expectation

2 What are our human limitations?

Mind, strength, ability.

READ
the passage

Read Hebrews 2:5-18, the chart "Lessons from Christ's Humanity," and the following notes:

❑ 2:9, 10   ❑ 2:10   ❑ 2:11-13   ❑ 2:14, 15   ❑ 2:16, 17   ❑ 2:18

3 Why is Christ worthy to be called "a perfect leader, fit to bring them into their salvation" (2:10)?

Because he was

4 What does Jesus call those who trust in him as their Savior (2:11-12)?

brother + sister

5 How do we benefit from the fact that Jesus shared in our humanity (2:14-16)?

He was tempted in all points as we.

6 Whom does Jesus help, and how does he help them (2:14-18)?

his believes,
He knows what they need from experience.

Jesus Christ is unique. He is God, greater than all the angels and creation. Yet Christ also became a human being and identified himself with our limitations. He is the one and only God-man. Jesus is able to save us because of his divine perfection. He was willing to save us by submitting to death on the cross and is waiting to save those who respond to him. His suffering not only created a way of salvation for us but also allowed him to identify personally with our struggles as human beings. Christ understands us because he has been human. Therefore, we can trust him not only for our salvation but for our daily needs—whether they are emotional, physical, or spiritual.

REALIZE
the principle

7 In what ways is Jesus, as a human being, like us?

flesh + blood.

8 In what ways is Jesus, as a human being, different from us?

Without sin

9 What happened to Jesus because he limited himself as a human being?

He gave
He still put the ear back on the soldier.   *Jh. 18:10*
                                                              Matt 26:53
                                                           X Luke
                                                              22:51

10 How is your faith affected by the fact that Jesus was a real human being?

None

11 How might the fact that Jesus was tempted help you cope with the temptations in your life?

He knows what it takes to live in this human body.

12 How might the fact that Jesus suffered help you cope with suffering? *Heb 2:10*

13 Jesus suffered so that we would benefit from God's grace (2:9-10). In what ways could we follow his example? How would doing so draw us closer to him?

14 What difficulties are you going through that you need to have Christ experience with you?

_____

_____

_____

_____

_____

RESOLVE
to take action

15 What would you like to say to God about your situation, knowing that Jesus understands?

_____

_____

_____

_____

_____

_____

A How did the Father honor Jesus because he suffered for us (2:8-9)? Who is affected by this? How are you affected?

B How did Jesus suffer? What would you say to someone who believes that God doesn't care about suffering in the world?

C Read the chart "Lessons from Christ's Humanity," but at the end of each line add the words "so I will . . ." and a personal application of that particular aspect of Christ's humanity.

MORE
for studying
other themes
in this section

LESSON 4
HARDENING OF THE HEARTS
HEBREWS 3:1-19

REFLECT
on your life

1 Finish these sentences:

A stubborn animal refuses to (or insists on) . . .

Follow

A stubborn politician refuses to (or insists on) . . .

listen

A stubborn coach refuses to (or insists on) . . .

Consideriry

A stubborn child refuses to (or insists on) . . .

authority

A stubborn Christian refuses to (or insists on) . . .

follow Christ teaching

READ
the passage

Read Hebrews 3:1-19 and the following notes:

❐ 3:7-15   ❐ 3:12-14   ❐ 3:15-19

2 Why was God angry with the children of Israel during their wilderness wanderings (3:7-11)?

Because they refused to do as He said

3 Why is it important for us to listen to God (3:7-11)?

He will lead us in the right direction

4 What is a hardened heart (3:8-15)?

Closed to advice or the truth.

5 How can we avoid turning away from God, as Israel did in the wilderness (3:12-14)?

Don't question His direction just follow.

It's easy to become insensitive to God. Spending a long time in a religious environment full of reminders about God can desensitize a person to God and his word. That's what happened to Israel as they traveled to the Promised Land. Instead of consistently listening to God and obeying him, they stubbornly insisted on going their own way. The author of Hebrews wanted his audience to learn from Israel's bad example. He wanted the new and growing church to be aware of the danger of stubbornness and to do what they could to remain sensitive to God's voice. A vital relationship with God needs constant renewal.

REALIZE
the principle

6 For what reasons do people's hearts become hardened against God?

They want their own way &
" make one wrong move the link to another,

7 Why is it important for us to remain sensitive to God and his word?

Satan is after us all the time and he jumps on just one on the first opportunity to mislead us.

8 What do stubborn people refuse to do (or insist on) regarding their relationship with God?

Free to make their own choices

9 What are the consequences of stubbornly refusing to do what God says?

Slavery and separation from God

10 What steps can a person take to renew his/her relationship with God?

Repent and be obedient !

11 What barriers will a person have to overcome to keep a close relationship with God?

Laziness + fleshly desires

12 What might be some personal warning signs of a growing hardness of heart?

Less prayer time + study of God's Word.

13 In what area of your life do you tend to take God for granted?

His Presence + direction

RESOLVE
to take action

14 What will you do to maintain a sensitivity to God and a willingness to obey him?

Talking to him and listening to his advice

A In what ways are Jesus and Moses alike (3:2-5)? How is Jesus greater than Moses (3:1-6)? What dangers exist when we confuse the servants of God with God himself? How can you follow your spiritual leaders without idolizing them?

MORE
for studying
other themes
in this section

B Who is God's household (3:2-6)? What does it mean to be a part of his house?

C What parallels exist between the challenges experienced by the people in Moses' day and the challenges we face today? What parallels can you find between the work Moses did for the people of Israel and the work Jesus did for the world?

LESSON 5
REST STOP
HEBREWS 4:1–5:10

We have entered our rest when we trust God to save us through Christ Jesus. We can not earn salvation so we are to rest.

Jews continued to offer sacrifices as long as they could.

REFLECT
on your life

1 What do you do to relax?

Set – anything that is not physical.

2 What's the most restful experience you can imagine?

Sit on the beach + watch the ocean.

READ
the passage

Read Hebrews 4:1–5:10 and the following notes:

❐ 3:11   ❐ 4:1-3   ❐ 4:4   ❐ 4:6, 7   ❐ 4:8-11   ❐ 4:11   ❐ 4:12   ❐ 4:13

3 Of the several possible meanings of *rest* explained in note 3:11, which ones are used in Hebrews 4?

x sabbath rest, daily rest,
x the promised land of Canaan,
x peace with God now + eternity.

4 Why didn't the people of Israel enter God's rest (4:2)?

Because of unbelief.

5 What's the connection between God's rest on the seventh day of creation and our rest (4:4-11)?

When our enter our rest it will be from our ~~the rest~~ ~~bodily~~ bodies rest,

6 How do God's word and God's sight contribute to our rest (4:12-13)?

God's word exposes even our thoughts + God sees + knows all things.

When God's word speaks of rest as a goal, it refers to two kinds of arrival. One is a relaxation created by knowing where life is going—security in who God is and what he has done for us. The other is the joy of finally getting there—eternal life after death. One rest leads right into the next. God has not designed life to be lived as a journey with an unknown destination. Rather, he has given his word to direct our journey and assure us of our destination. We choose to enter or reject the rest he offers.

REALIZE
the principle

7 In what ways is *rest* a good term to describe salvation?

We are not working to hopefully obtain salvation. In Christ we have already received and are just one step from eternity.

8 What does it mean for Christians to enter God's rest?

There is not given work to do, just be faithful to complete his design.

9 How is entering God's rest a partial experience in the present and a complete experience in the future?

We are saved, being saved & will be saved.

RESPOND
to the message

10 When do you tend to be anxious and uncertain about your faith?

There is always the unknown to be faced but we know we are just one breath away.

11 What response does God require of people today in order to enter his rest?

We Receive His Son as our saviour.

12 What is the clearest evidence in your own life that you have entered God's rest?

I have done what he asked me to do and I am staying faithful to the end.

RESOLVE
to take action

13 List truths about God that will help you relax and rest in what he has done for you.

Gods Word is eternal & true.
He has always done what he said

14 Ask God to remind you in frantic moments that you are trusting him with your life. Write down what you will say to him during those times.

In a fr frantic moment what would you like God to remind you all of that would be an assurance for you?

15 Write a brief prayer to God thanking him for the rest he offers.

MORE
for studying
other themes
in this section

A How is the Old Testament used in Hebrews 4? How can we learn from the Old Testament today?

B What is the importance of the word *today* as it is used in Hebrews 4:7?

C What is the purpose of God's word (4:12)? Using the symbol of an X-ray machine or a laser, describe how God's word functions in your life.

D On what does the author of Hebrews base the encouragement to "hold firmly to what we believe" (4:14)?

E Jesus "faced all of the same testings we do, yet he did not sin" (4:15). How can this be significant to you when you're facing temptation? How does it affect your prayers?

F In what ways is Jesus like any other human priest (5:1-3)? How is he remarkably different? How is Jesus your priest now?

G How do Jesus' actions as our substitute affect our relationship with God? How do those same actions help us cope with the challenges and temptations of this life? In what ways have you specifically experienced Christ's substitution for you?

H How was the death of Jesus an act of supreme trust (5:7)? What areas of your life do you need to submit to God more fully?

LESSON 6
GET GROWING!
HEBREWS 5:11–6:12

REFLECT
on your life

1 How have your tastes in food changed over the years?

none

2 If you could grow up again, what would you like to learn more quickly than you did the first time?

READ
the passage

Read Hebrews 5:11–6:12 and the following notes:

❏ 5:12, 13   ❏ 5:12-14   ❏ 5:14   ❏ 6:1, 2   ❏ 6:7, 8   ❏ 6:10   ❏ 6:11, 12

3 What are the "basic things" (or "milk") of God's word (5:11–6:2)?

4 What is a spiritually mature person like (5:12-14)?

_____

_____

_____

REALIZE
the principle

There are important differences between being *exposed* to the truth and *responding* to the truth. People can read the Bible and listen to sermons for years without ever internalizing God's truth. They know what God wants but never do it. The problem with the Hebrews was that they were still arguing about basic facts of their faith and not growing in their understanding of the Scriptures and their relationship with God. They knew what it meant to be saved but didn't know much about doing what was right. In effect, they were still spiritual babies. They needed to mature in their faith. How does this happen? Spiritual maturity comes from continually putting into practice the truths we have learned.

5 What role does knowledge play in the spiritual growth process?

_____

_____

_____

6 How does maturity come from action?

By doing what you know to do without
having to think about it

_____

_____

7 How does diligence contribute to spiritual maturity?

_____

_____

_____

8 What essential facts should a new Christian be taught in order to get a good start in spiritual growth?

_6:1~3_

_____

_____

Where do you fit on this scale?

RESPOND
to the message

9 Place an X on the scale to rate your present level of spiritual growth:

Unborn   Infant   Toddler   Child   Adolescent   Young Adult   Mature Adult

_____ _____ _____ _____ _____ _____ _____

10 What could you do to advance one level during the next year?

_____

_____

_____

_____

_____

11 What basic things listed in this passage do you still need to learn more about?

_____

_____

_____

_____

12 In what areas do you need help putting your faith into practice?

_____

_____

_____

_____

_____

List some specific answers to these two sides of growing:

RESOLVE
to take action

13 Ways I could learn more of what the Bible teaches:

_____

_____

_____

_____

14 Actions I need to take based on what I know the Bible teaches:

_____

_____

_____

_____

_____

A The Hebrew Christians were slow to learn (5:11). What were they to do about this? What can you do to accelerate your learning?

MORE
for studying
other themes
in this section

B How can a person be nailing the Son of God to the cross again (6:6)? How likely is it for a person who truly understands what Christ has done to turn away from him (6:4-5)? What is the evidence that a person has truly responded to Christ? How can this passage serve as a motivation for you to live for Christ?

C What were the Hebrew Christians doing right despite their immaturity (6:10)? How could they build on this, moving toward maturity? In what ways can you move toward maturity?

LESSON 7
A PRIEST FOREVER
HEBREWS 6:13–7:28

REFLECT
on your life

1 What are your minister's most important responsibilities?

Preaching the Word

Give a clear direction for the church.

2 What were some of the responsibilities of the Old Testament priests?

Representing the people to ~~the~~ God.

READ
the passage

Read Hebrews 6:13–7:28 and the following notes:

❐ 6:18, 19   ❐ 6:19, 20   ❐ 7:3-10   ❐ 7:11-17   ❐ 7:22-24   ❐ 7:25   ❐ 7:27
❐ 7:28

3 Identify the promise, the priest, and the plan being explained in this passage (6:13–7:28).

The promise is: *Bless thee & multiply you*

The priest is: *God Jesus Christ.*

The plan is: _____

4 What facts do we learn about God from this passage (6:13–7:28)?

_____

_____

_____

5 What characteristics of Jesus Christ make him the only acceptable High Priest for the entire human race (7:22-28)?

_____

_____

_____

6 What is Jesus' role as High Priest (7:25-28)?

_____

_____

_____

The author of Hebrews was captivated by an overwhelming thought—any way we look at Jesus, he is the greatest! Throughout this book the most cherished heroes, ideals, and systems in Jewish history are admired, then placed in proper perspective when compared with Jesus. What many had come to think of as God's plan was only a foreshadow of what was to come. The countless animal sacrifices represented the ultimate sacrifice of God's own Son. The generations of priests who served the people represented the one Priest who would save the people. Jesus was both the sacrifice and the Priest, and through him we can be forgiven and have access to God.

REALIZE
the principle

7 For what reasons is it important to remember that Jesus did not come to destroy the Jewish system but to fulfill it?

_____

_____

_____

8 What does it mean that Jesus "lives forever to intercede with God on their behalf" (7:25)?

_____

_____

_____

9 Why is it significant that Jesus sacrificed himself "once for all" (7:27)?

_____

_____

_____

10 How would the author of Hebrews want us to treat the Old Testament of the Bible?

_____

_____

_____

11 In what ways do you treat Jesus as high priest in your life?

_____

_____

_____

12 What does Jesus do for you personally as your high priest?

_____

_____

_____

13 How does this reality affect the way you live?

_____

_____

_____

_____

14 What change can you make in your life to reflect the truth that Jesus is your high priest?

_____

_____

_____

15 Use the following outline from Hebrews 7:26 for a prayer of appreciation for Christ's ministry in your life:

Lord Jesus, because you are . . .

holy, I can _____

_____

blameless, I can _____

_____

unstained by sin, I can _____

_____

set apart from sinners, I can _____

_____

in the highest place of honor in heaven, I can _____

_____

16 What is one thing about Jesus that you value more highly as a result of this study?

_____

_____

A Abraham had to wait for God's promise to be fulfilled (6:13-15). What promises are you still waiting for God to fulfill? How can you show your trust in God while you're waiting?

B How is the story of Abraham and Melchizedek in Genesis 14:17-20 used to point out the greatness and uniqueness of Jesus Christ? What other comparisons to Christ help you to realize how great he is?

C If the Old Testament law was not given as a guide for salvation, what was its purpose (7:18-19)? How does God speak to you through the Old Testament today?

D How are the Old Testament sacrifices for sin different from Christ's sacrifice for sin? What did Christ's sacrifice accomplish for you? How can you respond to what he did?

E What does it mean for one person to bless another? How does Hebrews 7:7 describe the nature of blessings? Who can you bless? How can you bless this person?

MORE
for studying
other themes
in this section

LESSON 8
DIRECT LINE
HEBREWS 8:1-13

Jn 10:17
25:1

I Chr. 1239

1 With what person in history would you most like to have a conversation?

REFLECT
on your life

_____

_____

_____

2 What would you discuss with this person?

_____

_____

_____

_____

_____

_____

Read Hebrews 8:1-13 and the following notes:

❑ 8:4   ❑ 8:8-12   ❑ 8:10   ❑ 8:10, 11

READ
the passage

3 What does the Bible mean by the word *covenant*?

agreement between two people

_____

4 What was wrong with the old covenant (8:7-9)?

Did not forgive sin

_____

_____

5 Why is the new covenant superior to the old (8:6, 10-12)?

_____

_____

_____

6 What happened to the old covenant after the new one was made (8:13)?

Was done away with + replaced with Christ.

_____

_____

A covenant is a promise between two people. Under the old covenant, God fulfilled his part of the promise by calling the Israelites his nation and leading them to the Promised Land. But the Israelites did not fulfill their side of the bargain. They continually turned away from God. So God made a new covenant with his true followers. This new covenant is far superior to the old. Under the old covenant, people depended on human means to access God—the Tabernacle, sacrifices, priests, and laws. Under the new, we can come directly to God through Christ, who opened the way for us to relate to our Creator personally and have our sins forgiven. Through Christ, God is present in us!

REALIZE
the principle

7 Why would the message of God's forgiveness be good news to the Jews?

_____

_____

_____

8 How has God fulfilled his part in the new covenant?

_____

_____

_____

9 What is our part in the new covenant?

_____

_____

_____

_____

RESPOND
to the message

10 What is the difference between knowing about God and knowing God?

_____

_____

_____

_____

11 How does a person come to "know the Lord"?

_____

_____

_____

_____

12 How do the words *ministers* (8:2) and *offer* (8:3) describe what Jesus does for us now? (Refer also to 7:25.)

_____

_____

_____

_____

_____

13 In what ways can you access God directly?

_____

_____

_____

_____

RESOLVE
to take action

14 If you don't know God personally, this would be a good time to begin that relationship. Who would be able to help you get started?

_____

_____

_____

15 If you already have a personal relationship with God, with whom could you share the good news of the new covenant?

_____

_____

_____

_____

16 What would be the best way to tell this person?

_____

_____

_____

_____

_____

A What does it mean for Jesus to be at God's right hand in the place of honor beside God's throne (8:1; see also 10:12-13)? What does it mean that he sat down? What is he doing as he "ministers in the heavenly Tabernacle" (8:2)?

B The Tabernacle was a copy of what was in heaven but not an exact copy (8:5). How can our churches today reflect the reality of Christ's work in heaven?

MORE
for studying
other themes
in this section

LESSON 9
REAL FORGIVENESS
HEBREWS 9:1–10:18

REFLECT
on your life

1 What makes it difficult for people to forgive someone who has really hurt them?

I don't think to many people plan on hurting someone, they for a moment think more of themself than the other person.

2 What makes it so difficult to ask another person for forgiveness?

Shame

Can you forgive but not forget?

READ
the passage

Read Hebrews 9:1–10:18 and the following notes:

❏ 9:6-8 ❏ 9:12-14 ❏ 9:13, 14 ❏ 9:15 ❏ 9:22 ❏ 9:24-28 ❏ 10:3
❏ 10:4 ❏ 10:5-10 ❏ 10:11, 12 ❏ 10:12 ❏ 10:17

3 What was involved in obtaining forgiveness under the old covenant (9:1-10)?

regulation for worship + where,
blood offered per sins
food + drink regulations and blood offerings were not able to cleanse of sins

4 How did Jesus change the way people could be forgiven (9:11-18)?

Christ became the great High Priest when He entered the great tabernacle in heaven and offered His own blood once for all time and secured our redemption forever.

5 What did Jesus' sacrifice do (10:1-8)?

Blotted out our sin once for all time. The old sacrifices reminded them of their sin and the need of a sacrifice.

6 What are the differences between the sacrifices of the old system and the sacrifice of Jesus (10:1-18)?

The old system reminded them of their sin but there was always a remembrance of sin. With Christ there was an offering of forgiveness once for all.

7 What has Jesus done with our sin (9:14-15, 22, 28; 10:10, 12, 18)?

He blotted out our sin and purified us, and there is no more need of a sacrifice again.
9:22
The old system made provision to cover sin but not to pay for it

Forgiveness costs. In order to forgive, our anger must be set aside, and a sacrifice must be made. But we who are hurt must make the sacrifice, not the one who hurts us. If we forgive a debt, it costs us money. If we forgive a wrong, it costs us the satisfaction of seeing justice served. The cost of sin is high. Under the old covenant, forgiveness cost the life of an innocent animal. Under the new covenant, it cost the life of Jesus. "Without the shedding of blood, there is no forgiveness" (9:22). The old covenant made provision to cover sin but not to pay for it. The blood of animals could not pay the high price—only Jesus could do that. He paid the full price once and for all, so he can completely take away all your sins. And when you're forgiven, you're free!

REALIZE
the principle

8 What's the difference between guilt and guilty feelings?

Having done a wrong,

Proven to have done a wrong.

9 How are people trapped by their sin?

No way to offer a sacrifice to cover & blot out sin
Sin still has its power on us but can not
destroy us or condemn us.

10 How can Jesus' forgiveness free us from our sin?

He cleanses us from sin once for all.

RESPOND
to the message

11 The yearly sacrifices under the old covenant were a constant reminder of sin that could not be taken away, leading to guilty feelings (10:3-4). What does Jesus' final sacrifice remind us of?

The price that God was willing to pay for our
sin to be forgiven and satisfied His demands.

12 What assurance do Christians have that their past sins are completely forgiven and taken away?

God gave us His Word that the blood of
Christ satisfied His requirement for our sins,
(all forgiven)

13 What prevents Christians from feeling forgiven?

Believing God's Word by faith that He would do what He said He would do.

14 How does the truth of permanent forgiveness affect the way you worship?

With praise & thanksgiving for God's precious gift of His only Son

15 Review your recent past, asking God to point out any areas in which you need forgiveness. Confess these sins to God as he reveals them to you.

RESOLVE
to take action

16 Many have found it helpful, following their confession of sins, to verbally accept God's forgiveness. Saying, "Thank you for forgiving my sins through Jesus" drives home the point that forgiveness does not depend on our efforts or our feelings but on what Christ did on the cross. Write a brief prayer thanking God for his forgiveness.

It is far better to live up grow in faith than to continue in rituals

A What are the unavoidable facts of life (9:27-28)? How do these facts affect the way you live now?

B What did God want from the Israelites more than sacrifices and offerings (10:4-8)? What implications does this have for our worship today?

C In what sense are we being made holy (10:14)? What is your part in this process?

MORE
for studying
other themes
in this section

Apostasy =
Gk- to express
   Abandonment of faith
A falling away;
a withdrawal
a defection   Matt 24; 10-12

LESSON 10
HOLD ON!
HEBREWS 10:19-39

R
REFLECT
on your life

1 What project has really stretched your limits of endurance?

Remodeling of 1st floor, after flood.

2 What kept you going?

The Lord + a few hard working people.

R
READ
the passage

Read Hebrews 10:19-39 and the following notes:

❏ 10:25   ❏ 10:32-36   ❏ 10:35-38

3 In Hebrews 10:19-25, the author noted five different ways to persevere. What are those five different ways?

1. Boldness before God
2. Full assurance of faith
3. Hold fast the profession of our faith
4. Provoke one another to love
5. Continue to meet together

4 When do Christians need to persevere (10:32-34)?

During times of afflictions

5 What can help Christians persevere in their faith (10:34)?

The care & love of others.

6 How can a Christian's confidence be rewarded (10:35-39)?

Continue to be confident in your faith, doing what God has gifted you to do.

The Jewish Christians were tempted to give up on their faith and go back to their old way of life. They were pressured and persecuted by the Roman culture and their Jewish brothers. It was easy for them to become disheartened. They needed encouragement to hold on to their faith. Today, believers still face the temptation to give up and give in. Whether it's the continual struggle with a nagging sin or persecution from an enemy, we will always have some opposition to our faith. But if we hold on and do the will of God, we will receive the reward he has promised.

REALIZE the principle

7 Why do Christians give up?

_Get tired and fell alone in the Lord's work.
Lack of self-control that they can say yes or no_

8 When might a person feel like giving up on his/her faith?

When personal failure has taken its toll on the mind, emotions & soul.

9 What does it mean to "hold tightly without wavering to the hope we affirm" (10:23)?

We have proved something to be true and worth dying for as Christ did for us.

RESPOND
to the message

10 When do you feel like quitting in your struggle against sin?

I have never do that, still have fights over sin but have never been overcome by it

---

11 How can believers encourage each other to persevere?

Fellowship, to encourage + support one-another; through prayer + contact.

---

12 How can the actions described in 10:19-25 help you hold on to your faith?

Jesus' death, burial + resurrection have provided the way to escape so great a temptation.

RESOLVE
to take action

13 What can you do this week to strengthen your faith?

Continue to stay in fellowship with Christ who is our all.

14 Whom can you encourage "to acts of love and good works" this week (10:24)?

_____

_____

_____

_____

15 What would be especially encouraging to this person?

_____

_____

_____

_____

_____

A What enables us to enter God's presence at any time (10:19-20)? What holds you back from talking to God about your deepest needs?

MORE
for studying
other themes
in this section

B What kind of person is referred to in Hebrews 10:26-31? Why would someone keep doing something that he/she knows is wrong? What's so dreadful about falling "into the hands of the living God" (10:31)?

faith + hope go together
1. It is firm persuasion + expectation that God will perform
all that he has promised to us in Christ.
(this fills us with joy unspeakable + full of glory.)
Christ dwells in the soul by faith, filling, and the soul
is filled with the fulness of God.
2. Faith demonstrates the the eye of the mind the reality
of these things that cannot be discerned by the eye of
the body.
It is designed to serve the believer instead of sight.
It is not a new invention, a modern fancy
It has been planted in soul of men ever since the covenant
of grace was published in the world.

2 parts of the grace of faith
1, It is the substance of
things hoped for.

2. It is the evidence of
things not seen,

One of the first acts of the articles of faith, which has a great
influence on all the rest was the creation of the world by the word
of God, from nothing! Ps. 33: 9 Out of no pre-existent matter.

v 4 - Paul now proceeds to set before us some illustrious examples
of faith in O.T. times, why does he not begin with our first parents, ?"

LESSON 11
FAITHFULLY HIS
HEBREWS 11:1-40

1 List the names of some people you trust.

REFLECT
on your life

_____

_____

_____

2 Why do you trust them?

_____

_____

_____

_____

_____

READ
the passage

Read Hebrews 11:1-40 and the following notes:

❏ 11:1 ❏ 11:3 ❏ 11:6 ❏ 11:13-16 ❏ 11:32-35 ❏ 11:32-40 ❏ 11:35-39
❏ 11:39, 40

3 Why do you think this chapter is referred to as the Hall of Faith?

_____

_____

_____

_____

_____

4 In your own words, what is faith (11:1)?

_____

_____

_____

5 How did the people profiled in this chapter show their faith (11:13-16, 33-38)?

_____

_____

_____

_____

6 Why were they willing to trust God (11:14-16, 35)?

_____

_____

_____

To encourage the first-century believers, the author of Hebrews reminded them of their tremendous heritage of faith. The men and women he listed had no guarantee of human reward and, in fact, often suffered terribly for their obedience. Yet they still trusted God and lived by faith. They were convinced that God had something better for them—if not in this life, then surely in the next. We have much more evidence of God's wisdom and love than they did (including Jesus, God's word, and even their examples), and we usually suffer much less. We have all we need to trust God today. How could we possibly doubt God's goodness?

REALIZE
the principle

7 How does a person demonstrate complete trust in God?

_____

_____

_____

_____

8 What motivated the men and women listed in Hebrews 11 to believe God?

_____

_____

_____

9 The men and women in Hebrews 11 were not perfect. What were some of their weaknesses and mistakes?

_____

_____

_____

_____

_____

10 What does God promise those who trust him?

_____

_____

_____

_____

RESPOND
to the message

11 In what ways is our life similar to the lives of those mentioned in Hebrews 11?

_____

_____

_____

_____

_____

12 In what ways is our life different from the lives of those listed in Hebrews 11?

_____

_____

_____

_____

_____

13 What evidence of faith is there in your life now?

_____

_____

_____

_____

14 What evidence do you have that God can be trusted?

_____

_____

_____

_____

15 What does God ask of you that will take faith to accomplish?

_____ RESOLVE to take action

_____

_____

_____

_____

16 Often we hold back from trusting God with certain areas of our life. What areas do you need to turn over completely to God?

_____

_____

_____

_____

A What evidence is there that God does not promise us heaven on earth (11:13-16, 35-38)? How might you need to adjust your expectations of God? What part does suffering play in living by faith?

B What three acts of faith did God commend Abraham for (11:8-12, 17-19)? What do his actions show about his belief in God? What was the basis for his trust?

MORE
for studying
other themes
in this section

LESSON 12
GET IN THE RACE!
HEBREWS 12:1-29

REFLECT
on your life

1 What would it take for you to get in better physical condition?

Kick in the rest of the pants.
Physical strength,

2 What holds you back?

Lazy, time,

READ
the passage

Read Hebrews 12:1-29 and the following notes:

❒ 12:1   ❒ 12:1-4   ❒ 12:3   ❒ 12:4   ❒ 12:5-11   ❒ 12:11   ❒ 12:12, 13

3 How is the Christian life like a race (12:1-3)?

4 Why is discipline an important part of a believer's relationship with Christ (12:5-11)?

Distraction will take us off or out of the race.

5 What kinds of divine discipline must Christians endure (12:7-11)?

6 What can we do to help others in their race (12:14-16)?

Encourage, walk beside them, Help them carry their load, Pray for them.

A successful runner recognizes the need for discipline as he/she prepares, participates, and perseveres in the race. To win requires working hard and enduring hardships. The author of Hebrews used the analogy of racing to illustrate an effective spiritual life. One reason the race is worth running well is because we do not struggle alone. Others have run the race and won, and their witness encourages us to run to win. What an incredible heritage we have!

REALIZE
the principle

7 What role does discipline play in the Christian life?

To keep our eyes focused on the goal line.

8 What can divine discipline teach us?

9 What five dangers can trip us up during the race (12:14-17)?

_____

_____

_____

_____

10 Describe what you think it might be like to arrive at the finish line described in 12:22-24.

_____

_____

_____

_____

_____

RESPOND
to the message

11 What stage of the spiritual race are you in right now—are you preparing, participating, or persevering?

_____

_____

_____

_____

12 What do you find most challenging about this stage?

_____

_____

_____

13 What responsibilities has God given you that you are complaining about, neglecting, fearing, or avoiding?

_____

_____

_____

_____

_____

14 How can God use discipline in your life as training?

_____

_____

_____

_____

15 Who can help you endure "divine discipline" (12:7)?

_____

_____

_____

16 What discipline will require endurance this week?

_____

_____   RESOLVE
                                                              to take action
_____

_____

17 Whom can you encourage to endure divine discipline?

_____

_____

_____

_____

A When might the struggle against sin involve giving your life (12:4)? Why is it important to struggle so hard against sin?

B In what ways are earthly fathers and our heavenly Father different (12:5-11)? What childlike responses does our heavenly Father require from us?

C What will happen to those who turn away from God (12:25)? What simple steps can a person take to avoid this?

D What will ultimately happen to the world (12:27-29)? What will last? How can these future events motivate us now?

MORE
for studying
other themes
in this section

LESSON 13
DON'T FORGET!
HEBREWS 13:1-25

REFLECT
on your life

1 What reminders do you have on your refrigerator, bathroom mirror, or calendar?

_____

_____

_____

_____

2 Of what do Christians often need to be reminded?

_____

_____

_____

_____

_____

READ
the passage

Read Hebrews 13:1-25 and the following notes:

❐ 13:1-5 ❐ 13:2 ❐ 13:3 ❐ 13:5, 6 ❐ 13:7 ❐ 13:8 ❐ 13:14 ❐ 13:17
❐ 13:18, 19 ❐ 13:20, 21

3 Of what did the author remind the Hebrew Christians (13:1-17)?

_____

_____

_____

_____

4 What *truths* or *principles* did the author mention (13:2-17)?

_____

_____

_____

_____

_____

5 What *commands* did the author include (13:1-24)?

_____

_____

_____

_____

_____

6 Why did the author put all these reminders at the end of his letter?

_____

_____

_____

_____

_____

The last chapter of Hebrews is filled with reminders. The author had explained many truths of the faith up to this point, and he didn't want his audience to forget that these should impact their lives in concrete ways. So he included a list to remind them what to do. Such reminders are important for us today as well. It is easy to forget or lose track of the responsibilities God has given us. Even people who have grown up in the church or memorized many verses need reminders of what God expects. *Remembering* what God has given us to do is the first step in *doing* it.

REALIZE
the principle

7 How do reminders to do God's will help us?

_____

_____

_____

_____

8 How do you respond when you are reminded of specific commands that you need to follow?

_____

_____

_____

RESPOND
to the message

9 What truths from this chapter had you forgotten?

_____

_____

_____

_____

_____

10 What commands from this chapter are good reminders for you?

_____

_____

_____

_____

_____

11 What changes can you make in light of what you've read in Hebrews 13?

_____

_____

_____

_____

12 How could you pass on some of these reminders to others in a way that will be well received?

_____

_____

_____

_____

13 Choose one of the reminders in Hebrews 13 that calls for a change in your life.

_____

_____

_____

_____

14 What action will you take this week in response to this reminder?

_____

_____

_____

_____

_____

_____

A What did the author of Hebrews want his audience to do regarding their leaders (13:7-8)? Who are your leaders, and what can you learn from them?

B What "strange, new ideas" were the Hebrews hearing about (13:9)? Why were the Hebrews susceptible to these ideas? To what kinds of strange ideas are people in your culture especially susceptible? As a part of your culture, what steps can you take to avoid being deceived by strange ideas?

C What kind of sacrifice can a Christian offer to God (13:15)? How can you offer this kind of sacrifice?

D Review all the lessons you've learned from the book of Hebrews. What changes in your life have these lessons made?

Evidence of Paul's authorship,

We much on signs & wonders, & miracles; + gifts of the H.S.

The message of sonship was special revelation given to Paul.

Death is the law of spiritual life — Rom 8:6